7 29

GW01079920

A Year of
Sundays

A Year of Sundays

Meditations on Christ, the Splendour of Eternal Light

Beda Brooks

Kevin
Mayhew

First published in 1994 by
KEVIN MAYHEW LTD
Rattlesden
Bury St Edmunds
Suffolk IP30 0SZ

ISBN   0 86209 547 6
Catalogue No: 1500010

Front cover: detail of Angel from
The Altarpiece of St Barnabas by
Sandro Botticelli (1444-1510).
Reproduced by kind permission of Galleria Degli,
Uffizi, Florence/Bridgeman Art Library, London.

Cover design by Graham Johnstone
Printed in Great Britain by
Redwood Books, Trowbridge, Wiltshire

CONTENTS

PREFACE

'The Spirit of the Lord God is upon me . . . he has sent me . . . to proclaim the year of the Lord's favour.' (Isaiah 61:1,2).

The fifty two meditations of this book are designed to encourage a deepening awareness that, as Christians, Sunday is our special day and that living out that awareness does indeed constitute a 'year of the Lord's favour'. Such may be our conclusion whether we start in sorrow or in joy for he is clothing us with 'the garments of salvation' and 'the robe of righteousness' (Isaiah 61:10). As we await the 'new heavens and a new earth' (2 Peter 3:13), our faith, hope and love may be steadily strengthened, and as they grow stronger so do we as people.

To begin, a sentence or so from one of the Gospels helps to direct our minds and hearts to Christ, perhaps his coming, his hidden or public life, his Resurrection or Ascension. This is followed by the prayer of Christ to be found in the psalms. In particular, it is hoped that this selection and arrangement of verses from the psalms will serve to enhance the capacity for praying the psalms in depth, and therefore assist not only those encountering them in the Sunday and weekday celebration of the Eucharist but also the increasing numbers of those reciting them in the Divine Office.

A 'Meditation' links the psalm verses with our own personal lives and the issues which surround us in the modern world, while silent prayer is also encouraged. Finally we recall that it is our joy and our privilege to praise Christ in whom we have been, are being and will go on being blessed 'with every spiritual blessing' (Ephesians 1:3); the Bible provides us with verses to express our praise of the God of love.

It is good to remind ourselves that Sunday is even more than the day on which the Father, the creator of the universe, 'rested from his mighty works, all things complete' and the day on which the apostles were filled with the Holy Spirit who 'leaped down in fire'. It is the very day on which Christ rose from the dead, the holy temple of his body being built once more just as he had prophesied. St. Maximus of Turin wrote:

> The light of Christ is day without night, day without end . . . the old gloom is dispelled by the endless brightness . . .
> Christ is the Son-day, to whom the Father-day has whispered the secret of his divinity.
> And so, my brethren, we ought all to rejoice on this holy day.

If we build the sanctuary of the Lord within ourselves and do so with special fervour on this most blessed day of his Resurrection, we will find his joy and peace.

These meditations may be a channel of grace at any time of the year, and may be repeated again and again so that new insights from the psalms may be discerned. Christian groups, communities and parishes may use them as well as individuals in their own homes or on private retreat. The companion volume, 'A Year of Fridays', may serve to focus attention on Christ's Passion and Death.

> O Rising Sun, you are the splendour of eternal light and the sun of justice. O come and enlighten those who sit in darkness and in the shadow of death.
> (Magnificat Antiphon, 21 December, the shortest day in the northern hemisphere.)

INTRODUCTION

'Although the whole of sacred scripture breathes the spirit of God's grace, this is especially true of that delightful book, the book of the psalms.'

The truth of St. Ambrose's words is evident when we search the psalter for the joy, peace and glory of Christ. The tools to be used in our quest include psalm verses into which we may gaze as into 'a mirror of tranquillity' and through which we may be granted 'a pledge of peace and harmony'. With sparks of divine love becoming enkindled within us we may also utilise another precious instrument, the silence of our own hearts. That constitutes a supremely positive tool, freeing us from superficial restlessness so that the Spirit may work in us and the Word may resonate through the very depths of our being. It is also encouraging to remember that the psalms were the very prayers Jesus prayed throughout his life.

The words of St Augustine, the great early fifth century doctor of the Church, may significantly deepen our prayer. He tells us that in the psalms

CHRIST PRAYS FOR US

AND

PRAYS IN US

AND

IS PRAYED TO BY US.

We must recognise that still today *Christ is praying for us as our Priest* since he is our eternal high priest who offered himself on Calvary for the forgiveness of our sins. We too form 'a royal priesthood' (1 Peter 2:9), set apart to sing the praises of God; we have been called out of 'a land of deep darkness' (Isaiah 9:2) into the luminous splendour of Christ.

Furthermore, *Christ is praying in us as our Head.* Thanks to the wonder of our baptism 'into Christ' we have 'put on Christ' (Galatians 3:27) and have become 'a new creation' (2 Corinthians 5:17). We who are many are members of his one body. It is therefore our delight to recognise his voice in us. Indeed, we are praying in him and he in us.

And who is Christ who is praying both for us and in us? He is the Word, and the Word is God; he is, in the words of the apostle Thomas 'My Lord and my God!' (John 20:28). Thus in the psalmist's verses *we are praying to Christ as our God,* one God with the Father and the Holy Spirit.

Praying the psalms is a means of intensifying our experience of Christ's presence within our own innermost being, an inspired way of listening with the ear of the heart, i.e. with increasing patience and sensitivity to the still small voice of the Lord. As we ponder, the verses truly become like a mirror to us. In them we see ourselves just as we are including our perception of our planet. The verses so nurture our souls that we can pray them (as John Cassian, a fifth-century monk, rightly suggests) as though we ourselves were composing them as our own personal prayer. The more Christlike we become the more pure will be our prayer. The psalms were fulfiled in Christ as he himself told his disciples on the road to Emmaus after his Resurrection, and today they are being fulfiled in us as we come to share more profoundly in the victory of the Risen Christ.

After asking 'what is more pleasing than the psalms?', St Ambrose wrote:

> In the psalms there is an opportunity for the people to bless and praise God; the psalms express the admiration that the people feel and what the

people want to say; in them the Church speaks, the faith is professed in a melodious way and authority finds a ready acceptance; there too is heard the joyful call of freedom, the cry of pleasure and the sound of happiness. The psalm soothes anger, frees from care and drives away sadness.

Can any Christian doubt that at this very time in world history and in our personal lives we need the psalms? That necessity may become our delight.

PUBLISHER'S NOTE

The psalms in this book are numbered according to the Greek Septuagint version and will normally differ from the Hebrew text by one number, as follows:

Greek Septuagint	Hebrew
1-8	1-8
9	9-10
10-112	11-113
113	114-115
114-115	116
116-145	117-146
146-147	147
148-150	148-150

The numbering of the verses also differs slightly as the title is incorporated into the body of the psalm.

In the beginning was the Word

THE WORD IN THE GOSPEL   John 1:1-4

In the beginning was the Word, and the Word was with God, and the Word was God. He was in the beginning with God. All things came into being through him, and without him not one thing came into being. What has come into being in him was life, and the life was the light of all people.

THE WORD IN THE PSALMS

Ring out your joy to the Lord, O you just.   32:1,6
By his word the heavens were made,
    by the breath of his mouth all the stars.

Before the mountains were born   89:2
    or the earth or the world brought forth,
    you are God, without beginning or end.
You founded the earth on its base,   103:5,6
    to stand firm from age to age.
You wrapped it with the ocean like a cloak.
Yours is the day and yours is the night.   73:16
It was you who appointed the light and the sun.
When I see the heavens, the work of your hands, 8:4-6
    the moon and the stars which you arranged,
    what are we that you should keep us in mind,
    men and women that you care for us?
Yet you have made us little less than gods.

In you is the source of life   35:10
    and in your light we see light.

Let all the earth fear the Lord,   32:8,9
    all who live in the world revere him.
He spoke; and it came to be.
He commanded; it sprang into being.

SILENT PRAYER

Christ Jesus is the Word of God, born of the Father before time began. He is our life today.

MEDITATION

The psalmists saw the heavens, not through the modern astronomer's space telescope, but with the naked eye. Yet, with the eye of their hearts trained on the invisible and ineffable heights they learnt reverential love for God, respect for all creation and a sense of humankind's destiny. With the unfolding of God's plan for our salvation we have come to know Christ as our life and light.

May the Word draw us to himself so that we may take our rest in him. May we focus our gaze on his wondrous plan to share with us nothing less than his divine nature, yes his very divinity. Lord, help us to appreciate how wonderful the soul is. With one single thought the soul can embrace heaven and earth and all in them. How much more beyond our understanding is the Word.

SILENT PRAYER

May our souls be perfectly recollected, and come to share in the divinity of the Word.

THE WORD OF LOVE   EPH 1:3,4,9,10

Blessed be the God and Father of our Lord Jesus Christ, who has blessed us in Christ with every spiritual blessing in the heavenly places, even as he chose us in him before the foundation of the world, and that we should be holy and blameless before him.

For he has made known to us in all wisdom and insight the mystery of his will, according to his purpose which he set forth in Christ as a plan for the fullness of time, to unite all things in him, things in heaven and things on earth.

'Mary, . . . you will conceive and bear a son'

THE WORD IN THE GOSPEL

The angel said to her, 'Do not be afraid, Mary . . . you
will conceive in your womb and bear a son . . . The
Lord God will give to him the throne of his father
David'.

THE WORD IN THE PSALMS

To you, O Lord, I lift up my soul.   24:1
For it was you who . . .   138:13-16
    knit me together in my mother's womb.
    I thank you for the wonders of my being,
    for the wonders of all your creation.
Already you knew my soul,
    my body held no secret from you
    when I was being fashioned in secret
    and moulded in the depths of the earth.
Your eyes saw all my actions,
    they were all of them written in your book;
    every one of my days was decreed
    before one of them came into being.

The Lord swore an oath to David;   131:11,13,17,18
    he will not go back on his word:
    'A son, the fruit of your body,
    will I set upon your throne.'
    The Lord has chosen Zion . . .
    'There the stock of David will flower;
    I will prepare a lamp for my anointed.
    I will cover his enemies with shame
    but on him my crown shall shine.'

Who can tell the Lord's mighty deeds?   105:2
    Who can recount all his praise?

SILENT PRAYER

Mary said: 'Be it done unto me according to your
word'.
Lord, may I also do your will.

MEDITATION

O King of David, fill the void of incompletion.

Christ is always willing to be conceived spiritually in
the hearts of those who yearn for him, and our longing
is in proportion to our emptiness.

May we deepen our appreciation of the wonder of
our being and that of our children who are signs of the
vitality of our society. Let us intercede for the unborn
and for those whose power threatens them. As
followers of Christ we stand for life, both biological and
spiritual.

Lord God, may we bring your Son to a perplexed
world in which the distinction between right and
wrong has become blurred. The responsibility is
awesome but, like Mary, let us cast fear aside.

SILENT PRAYER

Each morning may we put on Christ.
Let us live in his spirit.

THE WORD OF LOVE   Gal. 5:16a,22a,25

I say, walk by the Spirit . . . The fruit of the Spirit is love,
joy, peace, patience, kindness, goodness, faithfulness,
gentleness, self-control . . . If we live by the Spirit, let us
also walk by the Spirit.

'My soul magnifies the Lord'

THE WORD IN THE GOSPEL   Luke 1:46,47

And Mary said,
   'My soul magnifies the Lord,
   and my spirit rejoices in God my Saviour.'

THE WORD IN THE PSALMS

The Lord is in his holy temple,   10:4
   the Lord, whose throne is in heaven.

I will sing and make music for the Lord.   26:6
Indeed how good is the Lord,   99:5
   eternal his merciful love.
   He is faithful from age to age.
The love of the Lord is everlasting   102:17
   upon those who hold him in fear;
   his justice reaches out to children's children.
You keep your pledge with wonders,   64:6
   O God our saviour,
   the hope of all the earth
   and of far distant isles.
All those you protect shall be glad   5:12
   and ring our their joy.
You shelter them; in you they rejoice
   those who love your name.
You are loving with those who love you: 17:26
   you show yourself perfect with the perfect.

O sing a new song to the Lord,   95:1,2
   sing to the Lord all the earth.
   O sing to the Lord, bless his name.

SILENT PRAYER

Consider the wonderful things the Lord has done for us.
Mary received a child from heaven.

MEDITATION

Mary, having learnt at a remarkably early age the lesson of humility, her own nothingness, glorified the Lord of Love. Others, absorbed in divine love, are similarly gladdened by the melodious prayer of Christ flowing in perfect harmony through their whole being. May we grow in responsiveness to the inner voice of the Spirit and give ourselves entirely to the praise of our ever faithful and compassionate God.

In our society today many are lonely, sick and old. Lord, grant us the grace to bring them the joy of Christ's song, wondrously echoed by Mary. May we make time to visit, to write letters and to telephone those whose lives would be enriched by our caring touch.

SILENT PRAYER

May we love each other as Christians should, and have a profound respect for each other.

THE WORD OF LOVE   Zeph 3:14,15,17

Sing aloud, O daughter of Zion;
    shout, O Israel!
Rejoice and exult with all your heart,
    O daughter of Jerusalem! . . .

The King of Israel, the Lord, is in your midst;
    you shall fear evil no more . . .
The Lord, your God, is in your midst . . .
    he will rejoice over you with gladness;
    he will renew you in his love.

'He has shown strength with his arm'

THE WORD IN THE GOSPEL
Luke 1:46,51

And Mary said, '. . . he has shown strength with his arm, he has scattered the proud in the imagination of their hearts.'

THE WORD IN THE PSALMS

The Lord is high yet he looks on the lowly   137:6
    and the haughty he knows from afar.

O my strength, it is you to whom I turn   58:10,11
    for you, O God, are my stronghold,
    the God who shows me love.
Yours is a mighty arm, O Lord;   88:14
    your hand is strong, your right hand ready.
You save a humble people,   17:28
    but humble the eyes that are proud.
Show forth, O God, show forth your might,   67:29
    your might, O God, which you have shown for us.

Love the Lord, all you saints.   30:24
    He guards his faithful.
Upon you no evil shall fall,   90:10,11
    no plague approach where you dwell.
    For you has he commanded his angels,
    to keep you in all your ways.
Be strong, let your heart take courage,   30:25
    all who hope in the Lord.

I will bless the Lord at all times,   33:2,3
    his praise always on my lips;
    in the Lord my soul shall make its boast.
    The humble shall hear and be glad.

SILENT PRAYER

> Lord, alone I can do nothing.
> You do everything.

MEDITATION

A slip of a girl in enemy occupied territory was to become the Mother of God. The foolishness of God was wiser than human wisdom. In the final analysis the economic, technological and military strength of the superpowers is a supreme irrelevance. A boastful and cunning complexity will not save the world. The power of the Rising Sun increases in us in proportion to the shrinking Self. Let us both recognise and thank God for the strength of our simplest thoughts.

Lord, deepen our simplicity for that will lead us along the road of realism, true humility. We thank you for the humble and often hidden lives of so many Christians who are bound together in the mighty Mystical Body of Christ.

SILENT PRAYER

> Constantly seek his strength.
> Unify and simplify daily life.

THE WORD OF LOVE   1 Cor 1:26,27,29

Consider your call, brethren; not many of you were wise according to worldly standards, not many were powerful, not many were of noble birth; but God chose what is foolish in the world to shame the wise, God chose what is weak in the world to shame the strong . . . so that no human being might boast in the presence of God.

He remembered the oath
which he swore to Abraham

THE WORD IN THE GOSPEL   Luke 1:67-69,72-73

Zechariah . . . prophesied saying,
　　'Blessed be the Lord God of Israel,
　　for he . . . has raised up a horn of salvation for us . . .
　　to perform the mercy promised to our fathers,
　　and to remember his holy covenant,
　　the oath which he swore to our father Abraham.'

THE WORD IN THE PSALMS

I will give you glory, O God my King,	144:1
I will bless your name for ever.	
May the name of the Lord be blessed	112:2
both now and for evermore!	
O Lord of salvation, bless your people.	3:9

O children of Abraham . . .	104:6
sing a new song to the Lord	97:1,2
for he has worked wonders.	
His right hand and his holy arm	
have brought salvation.	
The Lord has made known his salvation;	
has shown his justice to the nations.	
God is made known in Judah;	75:2
in Israel his name is great.	

The Lord's friendship is for those who revere him;	24:14
to them he reveals his covenant.	
He remembers his covenant for ever,	104:8,9
the covenant he made with Abraham.	
Give thanks to the Lord for he is good;	117:29
for he remembered his holy word,	104:42
which he gave to Abraham his servant.	

SILENT PRAYER

> We are the people of the new and everlasting covenant.
> Lord, our hope is in you.

MEDITATION

The life of Abraham, like that of David, forms part of the history not only of the Jews but of all Christians. May we appreciate the marvel of salvation history, its revelation in the Scriptures and the new insights stemming from advances in Biblical scholarship. The secular history of our nations and of international relations can find ultimate meaning and fulfilment only in global salvation. Our vision embraces all time, and our lives are supported by a great heritage.

Lord, grant us the grace to make time for and to take delight in our Bible Reading. As we see how prophecies were fulfilled increase our trust in your promises. May neither apathy nor timidity prevent us from communicating our enthusiasm to others.

SILENT PRAYER

> May we change our world's history by living out your commandment of perfect love.

THE WORD OF LOVE   Deut 7:6,9

You are a people holy to the Lord your God; the Lord your God has chosen you to be a people for his own possession . . . Know therefore that the Lord your God is God, the faithful God who keeps covenant and steadfast love with those who love him and keep his commandments to a thousand generations.

'The Word became flesh'

THE WORD IN THE GOSPEL John 1:14,16

And the Word became flesh and dwelt among us, full
of grace and truth; we have beheld this glory, glory as
of the only Son from the Father. And from his fullness
have we all received, grace upon grace.

THE WORD IN THE PSALMS

The Lord said to me: 'You are my Son. 2:7,6
   It is I who have begotten you this day.
   It is I who have set up my king
   on Zion, my holy mountain.'
A prince from the day of your birth, 109:3
   from the womb before the dawn I begot you.

Yes, it was you who took me from the womb, 21:10,11
   entrusted me to my mother's breast.
To you I was committed from my birth
   from my mother's womb you have been my God.

Mercy and faithfulness have met; 84:11,12
   justice and peace have embraced.
Faithfulness shall spring from the earth
   and justice look down from heaven.
He shall descend like rain on the meadow, 71:6,7
   like raindrops on the earth.
In his days justice shall flourish
   and peace till the moon fails.
Let the peoples praise you, O God; 66:6-8
   let all the peoples praise you.
The earth has yielded its fruit
   for God, our God, has blessed us.
May God still give us his blessing
   till the ends of the earth revere him.

SILENT PRAYER

Such is our great need that we say:
Christ, our wisdom, enrich us still further from the
treasury of your grace.

MEDITATION

The Word was born complete in what is ours, sharing
our weaknesses, but not our faults. Such was his
compassion that the Invisible Lord of all made himself
visible to us and became totally one for us. By being
himself truly man and by pouring out the fullness of his
blessings upon us he helps us to receive God. The
mystery of Christ's glory is shining in our world. Let us
rest within ourselves by shutting out all that is not the
Word who is God.

What can we give you, O Christ, for you give all to
us? Let us offer our very selves in thanksgiving and
love.

May Christ, the desire of the nations, be proclaimed
to all peoples.

SILENT PRAYER

Glory to God in the highest. He will award the crown
of peace to all who long for his coming.

THE WORD OF LOVE   Phil 2:5-7,9-11

Let the same mind be in you that was in Christ Jesus,
who, though he was in the form of God, did not regard
equality with God as something to be exploited, but
emptied himself, taking the form of a slave, being born
in human likeness . . . Therefore God also highly exalted
him and gave him the name that is above every name,
so that at the name of Jesus every knee should bend, in
heaven and on earth and under the earth, and every
tongue should confess the Jesus Christ is Lord, to the
glory of God the Father.

Simeon came into the temple

THE WORD IN THE GOSPEL   Luke 2:27,28,30,32

Simeon came into the temple; and when the parents
brought in the child Jesus . . . he took him up in his
arms and blessed God and said, '. . . mine eyes have
seen thy salvation . . . a light for revelation to the
Gentiles, and for glory to thy people Israel.'

THE WORD IN THE PSALMS

There is one thing I ask of the Lord,   26:4
    for this I long,
    to live in the house of the Lord,
    all the days of my life,
    to savour the sweetness of the Lord,
    to behold his temple.
O that Israel's salvation might come from Zion!   52:7
When God delivers his people from bondage,
    then Jacob will be glad and Israel rejoice.

O Lord, I love the house where you dwell,   25:8
    the place where your glory abides.
The ends of the earth stand in awe   64:9
    at the sight of your wonders.
The lands of sunrise and sunset
    you fill with your joy.
We bless you from the house of the Lord;   117:26,27,25
    the Lord God is our light.
Blessed in the name of the Lord
    is he who comes.
O Lord, grant us salvation.

He has remembered his truth and love   97:3
    for the house of Israel.
He remembers us, will give us his blessing;   113:12,13
    he will bless the family of Israel.
The Lord will bless those who fear him,
    the little no less than the great.

SILENT PRAYER

May we be joyful in your house of prayer.
Praise the Lord in his holy church.

MEDITATION

As the child Jesus grew he came to burn with zeal for
the glory of his Father's house. We thank you, Lord, for
the grace-inspired achievements of architects and
builders who have created the beauty of our cathedrals
and churches. We thank you for those who have
enhanced our worship by their work in stained glass,
paint, metal and wood. May our liturgical celebrations
possess integrity.

Lord of Light which never fails, bless the 'little ones'
who do their best – the chorister who tries so hard and
the person who arranges the flowers so carefully. Grant
us the wisdom to see beyond any superficial
disturbance caused by another's insentitivity or
ineptitude. May all worshippers be united in a
symphony of peace and love.

SILENT PRAYER

When two or three are gathered in my name
there am I in their midst.

THE WORD OF LOVE   Sir 24:1a,3a,10-12

Wisdom will praise herself . . .
    I came forth from the mouth of the Most High, . . .
    In the holy tabernacle I ministered before him,
    and so I was established in Zion.
    In the beloved city likewise he gave me a resting
    place,
    and in Jerusalem was my dominion.
    So I took root in an honoured people,
    in the portion of the Lord, who is their inheritance.

27

Wise men from the East saw the star

THE WORD IN THE GOSPEL   Matt 2:10,11

When they saw the star, they rejoiced exceedingly with
great joy; and going into the house they saw the child
with Mary his mother, and they fell down and
worshipped him. Then, opening their treasures, they
offered him gifts, gold and frankincense and myrrh.

THE WORD IN THE PSALMS

The kings of Sheba and Seba,   71:10,11,15
    shall bring him gifts.
Before him all rulers shall fall prostrate,
    all nations shall serve him.
Long may he live,
    may the gold of Sheba be given him.

My heart overflows with noble words.   44:2,8-10
To the king I must speak the song I have made;
    my tongue as nimble as the pen of a scribe.
You are the fairest of the people on earth.
Therefore God, your God, has anointed you
    with the oil of gladness above other kings:
    your robes are fragrant with aloes and myrrh.
    On your right stands the queen in gold of Ophir.
All the rulers on earth shall thank you.   137:4,5
They shall sing of the Lord's ways:
    'How great is the glory of the Lord!'

Rejoice, rejoice in the Lord,   31:11
    exult, you just!
    O come, ring out your joy,
    all you upright of heart.
Praise the Lord from the heavens,   148:1-3
    praise him in the heights.
    Praise him, all his angels,
    praise him, shining stars.

SILENT PRAYER

And you, the stars of the heavens, O bless the Lord.
You shine steadfastly with grace-filled rays.

MEDITATION

The wise men were led by the star to the child. We share
their wisdom if we too seek Christ our king and with
interior joy adore him in the silence of our hearts. The
mystery of divine grace is shining like a star in our lives
and we are being entrusted with grace intended for
others. May we and all Christian evangelists lift up our
eyes on high. May we positively recognise that grace
and truth are found among those from different
cultures; let us always remember that these elements
constitute a secret presence of Christ.

Lord, grant that many constellations of grace and
truth may be revealed for all to perceive, and may we
follow you wherever you lead.

SILENT PRAYER

Behold our loving Redeemer and Mary, the Mother
of Fair Love.
May we guide others to you, O Lord.

THE WORD OF LOVE   Tobit 13:7,10,11

I exalt my God:
 my soul exalts the King of heaven,
 and will rejoice in his majesty.
Give thanks worthily to the Lord,
 and praise the King of the ages.
Many nations will come from afar to the name of the
Lord God,
 bearing gifts in their hands, gifts for the King of
heaven.

I called my son out of Egypt

THE WORD IN THE GOSPEL Matt 2:14,15

Joseph rose and took the child and his mother by night,
and departed to Egypt, and remained there until the
death of Herod. This was to fulfil what the Lord had
spoken by the prophet, 'Out of Egypt have I called my
son.'

THE WORD IN THE PSALMS

Israel came into Egypt.	104:23

O God, hear my cry!	60:2,3
Listen to my prayer!	
From the end of the earth I call.	
Your statutes have become my song	118:54
in the land of exile.	
O Lord, remember me	105:4
out of the love you have for your people.	
Long enough have I been dwelling	119:6
with those who hate peace.	
Come to me Lord, with your help	105:4,5
that I may see the joy of your chosen ones	
and share the glory of your people.	
Let me dwell in your tent for ever	60:5
and hide in the shelter of your wings.	

I am sure I shall see the Lord's goodness	26:13,14
in the land of the living.	
Hope in him, hold firm and take heart.	
Hope in the Lord!	

So he brought out his people with joy,	104:43,45
his chosen ones with shouts of rejoicing . . .	
that they might keep his precepts,	

that they might observe his laws.
Alleluia!

SILENT PRAYER

May the light of Christ guide us on our journey
through life

MEDITATION

Millions have been forced to leave their homelands due
to natural disasters or political and military upheavals.
The Holy Family knew the sorrow of exile; it was a
lived experience. Lord, bless refugees, migrants,
itinerant people and all suffering profound anguish of
soul due to separation from their families and
communities. We give thanks for all who joyfully return
to their homes and loved ones or find refuge and new
life among strangers.

Those Christians who are blessed with stable lives in
the land of their birth are also invited to leave the world
and its false values. As exiles from our heavenly
homeland our yearning for the vision of God should
increase. Help us, Lord, to make the psalms the song of
our exile; in them may we find nourishment and
medicine for our spiritual journey.

SILENT PRAYER

May we respect the rights of others and foster the
coming of your kingdom.

THE WORD OF LOVE   Exod 15:1a,2,11

Moses and the people of Israel sang this song to the
Lord, saying,
    . . . The Lord is my strength and my song,
    and he has become my salvation;
    This is my God, and I will praise him,
    my Father's God, and I will exalt him.
    Who is like thee, O Lord, among the gods?
    Who is like thee, majestic in holiness,
    terrible in glorious deeds, doing wonders?

The child Jesus was filled with wisdom

THE WORD IN THE GOSPEL   Luke 2:40

The child grew and became strong, filled with wisdom;
and the favour of God was upon him.

THE WORD IN THE PSALMS

How shall the young remain sinless?   118:9
  By obeying your word.
To fear the Lord is the first stage of wisdom;   110:10
  all who do so prove themselves wise.

O God, hear my prayer,   60:6
  grant me the heritage of those who fear you.
It was your hands that made me and shaped me: 118:73,34,
  help me to learn your commands.   66,64
Train me to observe your law,
  to keep it with my heart.
Teach me discernment and knowledge
  for I trust in your commands.
Lord, your love fills the earth.
  Teach me your statutes.
My lips will speak words of wisdom.   48:4
  My heart is full of insight.

O my Strength, it is you to whom I turn,   58:18
  for you, O God, are my stronghold,
  the God who shows me love.
I have more understanding than the old   118:100,32
  for I keep your precepts.
I will run the way of your commands;
  you give freedom to my heart.

SILENT PRAYER

Nothing is so valuable as the soul.
O my Strength, grant me the spirit of wisdom.

MEDITATION

Our children and adolescents are growing up in a world
whose values are often subversive to family life. Many
are more sinned against than sinning. All need a
wisdom beyond their years if they are to resist the
harmful pressures of a confused society. Being 'grown
up' does not mean total freedom; maturity is rather to
be seen as being proportioned to the completed growth
of Christ.

Lord, may our teenagers be inspired by
compassionate Christian men and women whose lives
are rooted in prayer. May adults be granted the grace of
listening and the spirit of understanding; may their
words bring light and wisdom. We also thank you for
the good example and spontaneous generosity of the
young.

SILENT PRAYER

Wisdom is an inexhaustible treasure, courteous and
proof against all error. Do not hide her riches.

THE WORD OF LOVE   Is 11:1,2

There shall come forth a shoot from the stump of Jesse,
and a branch shall grow out of his roots.
And the Spirit of the Lord shall rest upon him,
   the spirit of wisdom and understanding,
   the spirit of counsel and might,
   the spirit of knowledge and the fear of the Lord.

Jesus had been baptised and was praying

THE WORD IN THE GOSPEL
Luke 3:21,22

Now when all the people were baptised, and when Jesus also had been baptised and was praying, the heaven was opened, and the Holy Spirit descended upon him in bodily form, as a dove, and a voice came from heaven, 'Thou art my beloved Son; with thee I am well pleased.'

THE WORD IN THE PSALMS

The Lord's voice resounding on the waters,   28:3,4,3b,10
    the Lord on the immensity of waters,
    the voice of the Lord, full of power,
    the voice of the Lord, full of splendour.
The God of glory thunders.
    In his temple they all cry: 'Glory!'

The waters saw you, O God,   76:17
    the waters saw you and trembled.
It was you who opened springs and torrents.   73:15
You walk on the wings of the wind,   103:3,4,30
    you make the winds your messengers.
You send forth your spirit . . .
    and you renew the face of the earth.

O Lord, it is you who are my portion and cup;   15:5:
    it is you yourself who are my prize.
I bind myself to do your will.   118:31
Do not give Israel, your dove, to the hawk.   73:19

The Lord looks on those who revere him,   32:18
    on those who hope in his love.
He changes desert into streams,   106:35
    thirsty ground into springs of water.
'You who fear the Lord give him praise;   21:24
    all children of Jacob, give him glory.'

SILENT PRAYER

> May we be faithful to our calling.
> May we be totally committed.

MEDITATION

Jesus was praying. On so may occasions the evangelists refer to him praying, and that is the precious example he has given us. His life flowed from his prayer, and so it must be with us if we are to become sharers in his divinity as he wishes.

Let us recall the renewal of our baptismal promises at the magnificent Easter Vigil service. We are asked whether we reject sin, the glamour of evil and Satan, prince of darkness. Our response expresses our desire to eliminate the unreal from our lives so that we are free for the dynamics of truth; these are love of God and of others, all others.

Lord, may we live in the glorious liberty of God's children. We thank you for Sundays giving time and space for spiritual rebirth.

SILENT PRAYER

> Let us renew our baptismal promises in the depths of our heart.

THE WORD OF LOVE   1 Pet 3:21,22a

Baptism . . . now saves you, not as a removal of dirt from the body but as an appeal to God for a clear conscience, through the resurrection of Jesus Christ, who has gone into heaven and is at the right hand of God.

'Blessed are the poor in spirit'

THE WORD IN THE GOSPEL

Matt 5:1-3

Seeing the crowds, Jesus went up on the mountain, and when he sat down his disciples came to him. And he . . . taught them, saying: 'Blessed are the poor in spirit, for theirs is the kingdom of heaven.'

THE WORD IN THE PSALMS

Arise then, Lord, lift up your hand!   9,10:12
    O God, do not forget the poor!

The Lord listens to the needy,   68:34
    and does not spurn his servants in their chains.
The Lord protects the simple hearts;   114:6
    for the Lord has never despised   21:25
    nor scorned the poverty of the poor.
    From them he has not hidden his face,
    but he heard the poor when they cried.
He will have pity on the weak   71:13
    and save the lives of the poor.
The Lord takes delight in his people.   149:4,5
He crowns the poor with salvation.
Let the faithful rejoice in their glory,
    shout for joy and take their rest.
God gives the lonely a home to live in.   67:7
Blessed are they who put their trust in God.   2:12

Lord, you hear the cry of the poor;   9,10:17
    you strengthen their hearts.
Blessed those whom you choose and call   64:5
    to dwell in your courts.
We are filled with the blessings of your house,
    of your holy temple.

Blessed be the Lord who has shown me   30:22
    the wonders of his love
    in a fortified city.

SILENT PRAYER

Lord, help us to be empty so that we may be filled with the Spirit of the Holy One.

MEDITATION

Just as we find Christ in the psalms, so we discover him in the Beatitudes. He, boldly challenging the bloated self-righteousness of the Pharisees, faced the virtually certain consequences. Here, portraying himself, he shows us the true image of man formed in the likeness of God. Christ is supreme and ineffable loveliness, but we need poverty of spirit if we are to be able to surrender ourselves totally, perhaps apparently recklessly, to him. Travelling light, free from all that would eventually encumber us, is a great gift and we need to review our lifestyle constantly. Extras are dead weight.

Lord, help us to strip ourselves of material things so that we may be free for what is spiritual.

SILENT PRAYER

May our lives yield spiritual fruit.
How am I to change myself to become like Christ?

THE WORD OF LOVE   1 Cor 2:9,10

As it is written,
'No eye has seen, nor ear heard,
nor the heart of man conceived,
what God has prepared for those who love him.'
God has revealed to us through the Spirit. For the Spirit searches everything, even the depths of God.

'Blessed are the meek'

THE WORD IN THE GOSPEL

Matt 5:5

'Blessed are the meek, for they shall inherit the earth.'

THE WORD IN THE PSALMS

The Lord's is the earth and its fullness,	23:1
the world and all its peoples.	
Those blessed by the Lord shall own the land.	36:22

The Lord's is the earth and its fullness,   23:1
   the world and all its peoples.
Those blessed by the Lord shall own the land.   36:22

If you trust in the Lord and do good,   36:3,4
   then you will live in the land and be secure.
If you find your delight in the Lord,
   he will grant your heart's desire.

A little longer – and the wicked shall have gone.   36:10,11
   Look at their homes, they are not here.
But the humble shall own the land
   and enjoy the fullness of peace.

I look to the faithful in the land   100:6
   that they may dwell with me.
Those who walk in the way of perfection
   shall be my friends.
My eyes are always on the Lord;   24:15
   for he rescues my feet from the snare.
I keep the Lord ever in my sight: 15:8
   since he is at my right hand, I shall stand firm.
To those who revere the Lord   24:12,13
   he will show the path they should choose.
Their souls will live in happiness
   and their children shall possess the land.
The lot marked out for me is my delight: 15:6
   welcome indeed the heritage that falls to me!

SILENT PRAYER

> Let us listen to the pledge of future glory.
> Lord, we hope in you for grace and for glory.

MEDITATION

Those seeking to maximise profits grasp the world's resources with an avaricious hand. Mineral deposits and agricultural land are subjected to ruthless exploitation; while people, the most noble and sensitive of all God's gifts to the planet, are denied dignity. Totalitarian regimes violate this transcendent dignity of the human person. But the touch of the meek is gracious, tender and kindly, as is the touch of the Lord.

Father, help us to 'put on Christ' and walk in his way of perfection. May our vision be wise and gentle, and our whole life an epiphany of the magnificent and mysterious power of meekness which preserves our personalities from annihilating anger and our global environment from destruction.

SILENT PRAYER

> Jesus, meek of heart, help us to imitate you.
> Show us the pilgrim path we should choose.

THE WORD OF LOVE   Zeph 2:3a;3:12,13

Seek the Lord, all you humble of the land,
    who do his commands;
    seek righteousness, seek humility . . .
For I will leave in the midst of you a people humble and lowly.
They shall seek refuge in the name of the Lord,
    those who are left in Israel.
They shall do no wrong and utter no lies,
    nor shall there be found in their mouth
    a deceitful tongue.
For they shall pasture and lie down,
    and none shall make them afraid.

'Blessed are those who hunger and thirst for righteousness'

THE WORD IN THE GOSPEL

Matt 5:6

'Blessed are those who hunger and thirst for righteousness, for they shall be satisfied.'

THE WORD IN THE PSALMS

Make justice your sacrifice and trust in the Lord. 4:6

I waited, I waited for the Lord 39:2,3
   and he stooped down to me;
   he heard my cry.
He drew me from the deadly pit,
   from the miry clay.
He set my feet upon a rock
   and made my footsteps firm.

I will praise you, Lord, with all my heart; 9:2
   I will recount all your wonders.
Justice and right are the pillars of your throne, 88:15
   love and truth walk in your presence.
You upheld the justice of my cause; 9:5,4
   you sat enthroned, judging with justice.
See how my enemies turn back,
   how they stumble and perish before you.
May the mountains bring forth peace for the people 71:3
   and the hills, justice.
Happy the people who acclaim such a God, 88:16,17
   who walk, O Lord, in the light of your face,
   who make your justice the source of their bliss.

The poor shall eat and shall have their fill. 21:27
   They shall praise the Lord those who seek him.
   May their hearts live for ever!

SILENT PRAYER

May our hearts rejoice in the victory of the Risen
Lord, the Shepherd King. He is our Righteousness.

MEDITATION

New generations are weaving new patterns in the
perennial quest for justice, and let us rejoice in these
fresh initiatives where the threads of the warp and weft
are blending to form patterns which Christ is providing.
International relief organisations, apostolic religious
congregations and increasing numbers of lay
communities are responding to those suffering severe
deprivation or living on the margins of society.

Grant, Lord, continued physical, emotional and
spiritual strength to your labourers. May they take up
their positions with their eyes fixed on Christ; may they
trust in his victory on their behalf. Righteousness is
their cause and the ultimate triumph is certain.

Let us also intercede for all victims of injustice.

SILENT PRAYER

The Lord tries his chosen ones like gold in a furnace.
They will have a rich reward in heaven.

THE WORD OF HOPE   Rev 7:13-17

'Who are these, clothed in white robes?' . . . 'These are
they who have come out of the great tribulation; they
have washed their robes and made them white in the
blood of the Lamb. Therefore are they before the throne
of God . . . They shall hunger no more, neither thirst
anymore . . . For the Lamb in the midst of the throne
shall be their shepherd, and he will guide them to
springs of living water; and God will wipe away every
tear from their eyes.'

'Blessed are the merciful'

THE WORD IN THE GOSPEL

Matt 5:7

'Blessed are the merciful, for they shall obtain mercy.'

THE WORD IN THE PSALMS

Who shall climb the mountain of the Lord?   23:3
Who shall stand in his holy place?
Those who do not slander with their tongue;   14:3
   those who do no wrong to their kindred,
   who cast no slur on their neighbours.

The Lord is compassion and love,   102:8,11
   slow to anger and rich in mercy.
For as the heavens are high above the earth
   so strong is his love for those who fear him.
Our eyes are on the Lord our God   122:3
   till he shows us his mercy.
Because with the Lord there is mercy   129:7,8
   and fullness of redemption,
Israel indeed he will redeem
   from all its iniquity.

Remember your mercy, Lord,   24:6
   and the love you have shown from of old.
I trust in your merciful love.   12:6
   Let my heart rejoice in your saving help.
You, O Lord, will endure for ever   101:13,14
   and your name from age to age.
You will arise and have mercy on Zion:
   for this is the time to have mercy,
   yes, the time appointed has come.

SILENT PRAYER

> Lord, help us to lay aside petty and judgmental
> attitudes.
> Your mercy is unfathomable and inscrutable.

MEDITATION

When the Lord descended in a cloud and passed before
Moses, he proclaimed, 'The Lord, the Lord, a God
merciful and gracious, slow to anger and abounding in
steadfast love and faithfulness, keeping steadfast love
for thousands, forgiving iniquity and transgressions and
sin' (Exodus 34:6,7). Such indeed is our God. Today
political instability and the risk of nuclear and other
technological accidents speak plainly to us of billions in
need of divine mercy for mere physical survival.

Loving Redeemer, spare our planet. Grant that we
may show your compassion to others; may we carry out
the works of mercy in perfect fellowship, with neither
arrogance nor impatience nor discord.

SILENT PRAYER

> O Mary, Mother of Mercy, watch over us.
> Our hope is in our God for he is rich in mercy.

THE WORD OF LOVE   1 Pet 2:9-10

You are a chosen race, a royal priesthood, a holy nation,
God's own people, that you may declare the wonderful
deeds of him who called you out of darkness into his
marvellous light. Once you were no people but now you
are God's people; once you had not received mercy but
now you have received mercy.

'Blessed are the pure in heart'

THE WORD IN THE GOSPEL   Matt 5:8

'Blessed are the pure in heart, for they shall see God.'

THE WORD IN THE PSALMS

Lord, who shall be admitted to your tent	14:1
and dwell on your holy mountain?	

Those with clean hands and pure heart,   23:4
    who desire not worthless things.
Those who walk without fault;   14:2,5
    those who act with justice
    and speak the truth from their hearts.
Such people will stand firm for ever.
They shall receive blessings from the Lord,   23:5
    and reward from the God who saves them.
The Lord is just and loves justice: 10:7
    the upright shall see his face.
How good God is to Israel,   72:1
    to those who are pure of heart.

Give judgment for me, Lord; I am just   7:9,11
    and innocent of heart.
God is the shield that protects me,
    who saves the upright of heart.
May innocence and uprightness protect me: 24:21
    for my hope is in you, O Lord.

'What can bring us happiness?' many say.   4:7
Lift up the light of your face on us, O Lord.
O God, be gracious and bless us   66:2
    and let your face shed its light upon us.

SILENT PRAYER

Let us prepare a pleasant dwelling-place for the Lord
in our hearts.
May we find him whom our hearts desire.

MEDITATION

The very existence of contemplative communities
praying day and night in the heart of the church is a
challenge to the modern hyperactive world. God is pure
Spirit, and he is our Light and our Sanctification. If we
are to see him with the eye of the soul, our task is so to
develop that through his grace we have ourselves
completely under control, with characters stable and
guided by faith and reason. Blinded by the brilliant
radiance of the divinity we may feel ourselves in
darkness, but the darkness is pregnant with good. Just
one spark of Light will begin to illumine the way.

Father, may Christ the Son penetrate our very
personalities, showing us the value of eternal things;
may we be enabled to receive him at so deep a level that
we can transmit him to others.

SILENT PRAYER

O Lord, I seek more than a fleeting glimpse;
help me to look for you constantly.

THE WORD OF LOVE   1 Tim 3:16

Great indeed, we confess, is the mystery of our religion:
He was manifested in the flesh,
vindicated in the Spirit,
seen by angels,
preached among the nations,
believed on in the world,
taken up in glory.

45

'Blessed are the peacemakers'

THE WORD IN THE GOSPEL   Matt 5:9

'Blessed are the peacemakers for they shall be called
children of God.'

THE WORD IN THE PSALMS

I am for peace, but when I speak,	119:7
they are for fighting.	
Instruct me, Lord, in your way;	26:11,12
on an even path lead me.	
When they lie in ambush protect me	
from my enemy's greed.	
Happy those whom you teach, O Lord,	93:12,13
whom you train by means of your law:	
to them you give peace in evil days.	

I will hear what the Lord God has to say,   84:9
   a voice that speaks of peace,
   peace for his people and his friends
   and those who turn to him in their hearts.
The Lord will give strength to his people,   28:11
   the Lord will bless his people with peace.
See the just, mark the upright,   36:37,38
   a future lies in store for the peaceful,
   but sinners shall all be destroyed.
   No future lies in store for the wicked.

In festive gatherings, bless the Lord: 67:27
   bless God, O you who are Israel's children.
   To you may the Lord grant increase.   113:14
May you see your children's children   127:6,5b
   in a happy Jerusalem!

SILENT PRAYER

Peace I bequeath to you, my own peace I give you.
His name is Wonderful Counsellor, Prince of Peace.

MEDITATION

The proliferation of nuclear weapons and the accumulation of arms by communities with fanatical leaders cannot but alarm. Let us respond by cultivating the peace of Christ within our own hearts; may we do so on this very day with such an intensity that it will influence our behaviour in moments of temptation. May we turn the other cheek when we are hurt by others, repaying abuse with courtesy. May Christians play their full part as citizens holding societies together.

Lord God, we long for world peace and so we join our minute daily sacrifices to the redeeming sacrifice of Christ who is your Son and our King and Peacemaker.

We thank you for peaceful homes and quiet dwellings.

SILENT PRAYER

You, therefore, must be perfect, as your heavenly Father is perfect.

THE WORD OF LOVE   Is 2:4

He shall judge between the nations,
    and shall decide for many peoples;
and they shall beat their swords into ploughshares,
    and their spears into pruning hooks;
nation shall not lift up sword against nation,
    neither shall they learn war any more.

'Our Father . . . hallowed be thy name'

THE WORD IN THE GOSPEL   Matt 6:9

'Pray then like this:
    Our Father who art in heaven
    hallowed be thy name . . .'

THE WORD IN THE PSALMS

I through the greatness of your love   5:8
    have access to your house.
I bow down before your holy temple,
    filled with awe.
'Long ago you founded the earth   101:26-28
    and the heavens are the work of your hands.
They will perish but you will remain.
They will all wear out like a garment.
You will change them like clothes that are changed.
But you neither change nor have an end.'
Lord, your name stands for ever,   134:13
    unforgotten from age to age.

Cry out with joy to God all the earth,   65:1-4
O sing to the glory of his name.
O render him glorious praise.
Say to God:
    'How tremendous your deeds!
    Before you all the earth shall bow;
    shall sing to you, sing to your name!'
How great is your name, O Lord our God,   8:10
    through all the earth!
May this song make your name   44:18
    for ever remembered.
    May the peoples praise you from age to age.

Silent Prayer

May we live as temples of God and praise his name
unceasingly.

Meditation

We cannot help being saddened when we hear the
Lord's name dishonoured and we are aware too that the
day of the Lord is often disregarded. Let us join with
Christ in giving honour to our Father: this we may do
through our eucharistic celebrations, prayer, spiritual
reading and a sensitive appreciation of the beauty of his
creation.

Let us ponder on the Father's majestic power and his
tender love, his presence in heaven and our desire to be
with him.

Lord Jesus, help us to make the Father known, loved
and honoured. May his holiness shine in us. We thank
you for the gift of Sundays, days making their
distinctive contribution to the well-being of society.

Silent Prayer

I will put my spirit into you.
Be holy as I am holy, says the Lord.

The Word Of Love   Mal 1:11

From the rising of the sun to its setting my name is
great among the nations and in every place incense is
offered to my name, and a pure offering; for my name is
great among the nations, says the Lord of hosts.

49

'Thy kingdom come'

THE WORD IN THE GOSPEL   Matt 6:9,10

'Pray then like this . . .
   Thy kingdom come,
   Thy will be done,
   on earth as it is in heaven . . .'

THE WORD IN THE PSALMS

It is you whom I invoke, O Lord.   5:3
In the morning you hear me;
   in the morning I offer you my prayer,
   watching and waiting.

Our God is in the heavens;   113:3
   he does whatever he wills.
A mighty God is the Lord,   94:3,5
   a great king above all gods.
To him belongs the sea for he made it.
God is king of all the earth,   46:8,9
   sing praise with all your skill.
God reigns on his holy throne.

His ways are faithfulness and love;   24:10
   for those who keep his covenant and will.
Let the heavens rejoice and earth be glad,   95:11,12
   let the land and all it bears rejoice.

Blessed are you, O Lord;   118:12,15,24
   I will ponder all your precepts.
Your will is my delight;
   your statutes are my counsellors.
Teach me to do your will   142:10
   for you, O Lord, are my God.
Let your good spirit guide me
   in ways that are level and smooth.
You will guide me by your counsel   72:24
   and so you will lead me to glory.

SILENT PRAYER

As we pray may mind and heart and voice be in
harmony.
May our personalities be held and unified.

MEDITATION

The Lord fills heaven and earth, holding all things in
unity. In him we live. He hears our prayer, whether recited
in a world-famous cathedral crowded with worshippers
or a solitary wordless yearning in a hidden place.

Father, may the power of evil in our universe be
broken and all be wondrously made new in the person of
your beloved Son, the king and centre of all hearts. May
all serve you in true freedom, willing what you will and
not running away from the challenge of being Christians
in our present environment. We acknowledge that it is
precisely those who do your will who will enter the
kingdom.

It is stunningly close; it is within.

SILENT PRAYER

Come, you blessed of my Father, inherit the kingdom
prepared for you from the beginning of the world.

THE WORD OF LOVE   Rev 19:5-8

And from the throne came a voice, crying,
    'Praise our God, all you his servants,
    you who fear him, small and great.'
Then I heard what seemed to be the voice of a great
multitude . . . crying,
    'Hallelujah! For the Lord our God the Almighty reigns.
    Let us rejoice and exult and give him the glory,
    for the marriage of the Lamb has come,
    and his Bride has made herself ready;
    it was granted for her to be clothed with fine linen,
    bright and pure –
    for the fine linen is the righteous deeds of the saints.

'Daily bread'

THE WORD IN THE GOSPEL   Matt 9:9,11

'Pray then like this . . .
    Give us this day our daily bread . . .'

THE WORD IN THE PSALMS

I am the Lord your God,   80:11
    who brought you from the land of Egypt.
Open wide your mouth and I will fill it.

You make . . .   103:14,15
    the plants to serve our needs,
    that we may bring forth bread from the earth
    and wine to cheer our hearts;
    oil, to make our faces shine
    and bread to strengthen our hearts.
You care for the earth, give it water,   64:10,12-14
    you fill it with riches.
You crown the year with your goodness.
    The hills are girded with joy . . . yes, they sing.

May corn be abundant in the land   71:16
    to the peaks of the mountains.
Let our barns be filled to overflowing   143:13
    with crops of every kind.
The Lord will make us prosper   84:13
    and our earth shall yield its fruit.
Happy the people with such blessings;   143:15
    happy the people whose God is the Lord.

SILENT PRAYER

    See in the bread Christ's body which hung upon the
    Cross and in the cup the blood which flowed from
    his side.

MEDITATION

If our personalities are to develop and be blended into a harmonious Christlike whole we need nourishment for body, spirit and soul. Well-balanced people make a well-balanced world. We pray for famine victims suffering a subhuman existence in our world; Lord, grant them their daily bread.

We thank you for those things which nurture the spirit – music, literature, art, architecture, the beauty of the countryside. Though varying in degrees of importance from one person to another we all savour their delights.

Our greatest need is to encounter Christ, the loving unified personality of God made man, and so we give thanks for the Eucharist. This great sacrament administers the medicine of immortality, heals our spiritual ills and nurtures the sharing of Christ's divinity.

SILENT PRAYER

In the Eucharistic banquet we celebrate the surpassing love which Christ showed in his passion.

THE WORD OF LOVE   Wis 16:20

Thou didst give thy people the food of angels,
and without their toil thou didst supply them from
heaven with bread ready to eat,
providing every pleasure suited to every taste.

Treasure in the heavens

THE WORD IN THE GOSPEL
Luke 12:33,34

' . . . Provide yourselves . . . with a treasure in the heavens that does not fail, where no thief approaches and no moth destroys. For where your treasure is, there will your heart be also.'

THE WORD IN THE PSALMS

The decrees of the Lord are truth
    and all of them just. 18:10-12
They are more to be desired than gold,
    than the purest of gold.
So in them your servant finds instruction;
    great reward is in their keeping.

Do not fear when others grow rich
    when the glory of their house increases. 48:17,18
They take nothing with them when they die,
    their glory does not follow them below.
Do not set your heart on riches
    even when they increase. 61:11
For the rich cannot buy their own ransom,
    or pay a price to God for their lives. 48:8-10
The ransom of their soul is beyond them.
    They cannot buy life without end,
    nor avoid coming to the grave.

In you, O Lord, I take refuge. 70:1
I gaze on you in the sanctuary 62:3
    to see your strength and your glory.
Bend my heart to your will 118:36
    and not to love of gain.
My soul clings to you; 62:9
    your right hand holds me fast.

SILENT PRAYER

The Lord cares for us in our need.
May our love be carefree and joyful.

MEDITATION

This is a time for turning our backs on the dazzling, but spiritually impoverishing, affluence of the world. Treasure in heaven may be accumulated with childlike simplicity; it consists of a multitude of small coins, the little daily sacrifices required if we are truly to love others and to risk opening ourselves to being hurt by others. Let us cling to a grace-inspired desire to love Jesus, our true treasure; the less we seek created things, the more we may absorb of the spirit of Christ.

Lord, grant us the grace to disregard our own feelings of discouragement; may we focus the will on the profound mysteries of Christ. In his heart are contained all the treasures of wisdom and understanding.

SILENT PRAYER

Lives of poverty and humility reflect the image of Christ.
May our hearts truly be with him.

THE WORD OF LOVE   Eph 3:14,16-19

I bow my knees before the Father . . . that according to the riches of his glory he may grant you to be strengthened with might through his Spirit in the inner man, and that . . . Christ may dwell in your hearts through faith; that you, being rooted and grounded in love, may have power to comprehend with all the saints what is the breadth and length and height and depth and to know the love of Christ which surpasses knowledge, that you may be filled with all the fullness of God.

'Seek and you will find'

Matt 7:7
THE WORD IN THE GOSPEL

'Ask, and it shall be given you; seek, and you will find;
knock, and it will be opened to you.'

THE WORD IN THE PSALMS

From heaven the Lord looks down   13:2
    on the people of the earth
    to see if any are wise,
    if any seek God.

O Lord, hear my voice when I call;   26:7,8
    have mercy and answer.
Of you my heart has spoken:
    'Seek his face.'
Those who know your name will trust you: 9:11
    you will never forsake those who seek you.
Your promise is tried in the fire,   118:140
    the delight of your servant.
Let the hearts that seek the Lord rejoice.   104:3,4
Consider the Lord and his strength;
    constantly seek his face.
O let there be rejoicing and gladness   39:17
    for all who seek you.
Let them ever say: 'The Lord is great',
    who love your saving help.
Let them say for ever: 'God is great',   69:5
    who love your saving help.

It is the Lord who grants favours to those whom he
    loves,   4:4
the Lord hears me whenever I call him.

SILENT PRAYER

    Ask, and it will be given you.
    Knock, and it will be opened to you.

MEDITATION

Our Saviour's encouraging words are deeply expressive of his love for us. We who share in his divine nature are to see his own dear face. We are not to search in vain; he has not hidden himself in some dark place.

The quest for power, prestige and possessions has reached epidemic proportions, but the Christian must be neither despondent about our world nor drawn to whatever will gratify self-centredness. If we pursue integrity we are seeking the Lord. The search, it is good to remember, is two-fold: there is the Lord's search for us and our desire for him. The finding is full of joy.

Lord, help us to go beyond ourselves by deeper prayer and more compassionate daily living. May we appreciate how the quality of each is intimately interconnected.

SILENT PRAYER

Seek and you will find.
May we walk with integrity and fix our gaze entirely on Christ, our beloved Redeemer.

THE WORD OF LOVE   Col 3:1,2

If then you have been raised with Christ, seek the things that are above, where Christ is, seated at the right hand of God. Set your mind on things that are above, not on things that are on earth.

Water welling up to eternal life

John 4:14

'Whoever drinks of the water that I shall give him will
never thirst; the water that I shall give him will become
in him a spring of water welling up to eternal life.'

THE WORD IN THE PSALMS

The waters of a river give joy to God's city, 45:5
    the holy place where the Most High dwells.

Some wandered in the desert, in the wilderness. 106:4-6
Hungry they were and thirsty;
    their soul was fainting within them.
Then they cried to the Lord in their need
    and he rescued them from their distress.
He pierced the rock to give them water; 104:41,42
    it gushed forth in the desert like a river
    for he remembered his holy word.
He satisfies the thirsty soul. 106:9

O God, you are my God, for you I long; 62:2
    for you my soul is thirsting.
My body pines for you
    like a dry, weary land without water.

My soul shall be filled as with a banquet, 62:6,4,5
    my mouth shall praise you with joy.
Your love is better than life,
    my lips will speak your praise.
So I will bless you all my life,
    in your name I will lift up my hands.
    'For the poor who are oppressed and the needy who
groan 11:6
    I myself will arise,' says the Lord.
    'I will grant them the salvation for which they thirst.'

Silent Prayer

Jesus loves us with an everlasting love.
Heart of Jesus, fountain of life and holiness, have
mercy on us.

Meditation

The multi-coloured, effervescent and intoxicating wells of
the world have the capacity to provide enticing pleasures.
Soon they are dried up; the thirst is unquenched. Our real
yearning is not for the finite, mere temporary diversions,
but for the infinite, the fountain of life, grace upon grace,
welling up within our souls from the moment of baptism.
Let us distinguish between that which anaesthetises and
that which truly satisfies.

Fountain of Eternal Wisdom, to you we draw near.
O splendour of eternal light and likeness of the substance
of God, cleanse us from all stain of sin; in your loving
kindness may we taste the pure, soothing and
strengthening waters of salvation. May we drink in with
delight whatever gives us knowledge and understanding
of you.

Silent Prayer

If any one thirsts let him come to me and drink.
Thus we believers receive the Spirit.

The Word Of Love   Is 12:3-5

With joy you will draw water from the wells of salvation.
And you will say in that day:
    'Give thanks to the Lord,
      call upon his name;
    make known his deeds among the nations,
      proclaim that his name is exalted.
    Sing praises to the Lord, for he has done gloriously;
      let this be known in all the earth.'

'My burden is light'

THE WORD IN THE GOSPEL   Matt 11:28,30

'Come to me, all who labour and are heavy laden, and I
will give you rest. For my yoke is easy, and my burden
is light.'

THE WORD IN THE PSALMS

Entrust your cares to the Lord   54:23,24
    and he will support you.
He will never allow
    the just one to stumble.
O Lord, I will trust in you.

In God is my safety and glory,   61:8,9,2
    the rock of my strength.
Take refuge in God all you people.
Trust him at all times.
Pour out your hearts before him
    for God is our refuge.
In God alone is my soul at rest;
    my help comes from him.
His own designs shall stand for ever,   32:11
    the plans of his heart from age to age.

You do not ask for holocaust and victim.   39:7-9
Instead, here am I.
In the scroll of the book it stands written
    that I should do your will.
My God, I delight in your law
    in the depth of my heart.

He will search who searches the mind   63:7
    and knows the depths of the heart.
May the Lord be blessed day after day.   67:20
    He bears our burden, God our saviour.

SILENT PRAYER

Learn from me for I am gentle and lowly in heart
and you will find rest for your souls.

MEDITATION

This wonderfully sustained text helps us assess our
personal problems. Labouring uphill in an environment
hostile to Christianity is no cause for depression even
when thousands appear to be pulling downhill. Calvary
is the mountain of the Beloved. 'Here I am, Lord,' but I
am not alone. You too, my Jesus, say in the fullness of
truth: 'Here I am'. With you to support me your
strength can find perfect expression in my weakness.
Hitherto undreamt of horizons open before me. With
even me as a Simon of Cyrene to support you so that
the burden will not be crushing.

Son of the Eternal Father, fill us with that abundant
grace that flows from your Sacred Heart.

SILENT PRAYER

We will find the God of love where there is loving
kindness.
May our souls rise to a new vision.

THE WORD OF LOVE   Jer 31:33

This is the covenant which I will make with the house
of Israel after those days, says the Lord: I will put my
law within them, and I will write it upon their hearts;
and I will be their God, and they shall be my people.

One who understands the word yields a hundredfold

THE WORD IN THE GOSPEL

Matt 13:23

'As for what was sown on good soil, this is he who hears the word and understands it, he indeed bears fruit, and yields, in one case a hundredfold, in another sixty, and in another thirty.'

THE WORD IN THE PSALMS

Alleluia!

111:1,2,6

Happy are those who fear the Lord,
    who take delight in all his commands.
Their descendants shall be powerful on earth;
    the children of the upright are blessed.
The just will never waver:
    they will be remembered for ever.

Happy indeed are those

1:1-3

    who follow not the counsel of the wicked;
    but whose delight is the law of the Lord
    and who ponder his law day and night.
They are like a tree that is planted
    beside the flowing waters,
    that yields its fruit in due season
    and whose leaves shall never fade;
    and all that they do shall prosper.
The just will flourish like the palm-tree

91:13-15

    and grow like a Lebanon cedar.
They will flourish in the courts of our God,
    still bearing fruit, when they are old.

Praise the Lord from the earth.

148:7,14

He exalts the strength of his people.

He is the praise of all his saints,
of the sons of Israel,
of the people to whom he comes close.
Alleluia!

Silent Prayer

Prayer makes the ground fertile.
Gracious Lord, forgive us our apathy and help us to
make friends of the saints.

Meditation

Alas, mediocrity comes more comfortably than
excellence. Yet, let us never forget our friends, the saints,
whose lives still continue to bear a hundredfold. With so
many witnesses from the past centuries to encourage us
and intercede for us, let us endeavour to live out a total
Christian commitment.

Lord, grant us a sense of proportion about the
meaning, duration and nature of our trials when set
against a glorious eternity in which all comes to
perfection in the fullness of Christ. We thank you for the
saints and for the manifold ways in which Christians
witness to Christ in today's world.

Following in the footsteps of the saints, let us
remember that even now we savour the delights of a
world beyond time and space.

Silent Prayer

May prayer possess an inner reality.
How may I yield a hundredfold?

The Word Of Love   John 15:7,8,11

If you abide in me, and my words abide in you, ask
whatever you will, and it shall be done for you. By this
my Father is glorified, that you bear much fruit, and so
prove to be my disciples . . . These things I have spoken to
you, that my joy may be in you, and that your joy may be
full.

'Winds and sea obey him'

THE WORD IN THE GOSPEL   Matt 8:26,27

And he said to them, 'Why are you afraid, you of little
faith?' Then he got up and rebuked the winds and the
sea; and there was a dead calm. They were amazed,
saying, 'What sort of man is this, that even the winds
and sea obey him?'

THE WORD IN THE PSALMS

There is the sea, vast and wide,   103:25
    with its moving swarms past counting,
    living things great and small.
Deep is calling on deep,   41:8
    in the roar of waters.

He stilled the storm to a whisper: 106:29,30,32
    all the waves of the sea were hushed.
They rejoiced because of the calm
    and he led them to the haven they desired.
Let them exalt him in the gathering of the people
    and praise him in the meetings of the elders.
'If the Lord had not been on our side,'   123:1,4,5
    this is Israel's song,
    '. . . Then would the waters have engulfed us;
    the torrent gone over us;
    over our heads would have swept
    the raging waters.'

Let the sea and all within it thunder praise.   95:11
Greater than the roar of mighty waters,   92:4
    more glorious than the surgings of the sea,
    the Lord is glorious on high.

O Lord God of host, who is your equal?   88:9,10
    It is you who rule the sea in its pride;
    it is you who still the raging of its waves.

Silent Prayer

Lord, may our faith increase. Enlarge the narrowness
of human vision.
May we be more responsive to your divine word.

Meditation

The power of Christ's divinity is revealed. Let us not
doubt that he is the Almighty One who can calm our
spiritual tempests. May we approach him with
reverential awe wisely conscious of his loving plan for
us. Our personal problems serve a purpose. Let us take
our stand with and in Christ since we know that all has
been revealed in him. Our Saviour will make all
manifest to us; our confidence gives him great joy. The
church may be storm-tossed through the centuries, but
even with sinful landlubbers on board it is seaworthy.

Lord, we acknowledge that our spiritual difficulties
are an absolutely necessary purification, and on calmer
days help us to increase the strength of our souls.

Silent Prayer

Listen we must, whether becalmed or storm-tossed.
Lord of Power, your word is all.

The Word Of Love   Dan 3:43,56,68

Bless the Lord, all winds,
 sing praise to him and highly exalt him for ever.
Bless the Lord, seas and rivers,
 sing praise to him and highly exalt him for ever.
Bless him, all who worship the Lord, and God of gods,
 sing praise to him and give thanks to him,
 for his mercy endures for ever.

'Your sins are forgiven'

THE WORD IN THE GOSPEL   Matt 9:2

Behold, they brought to him a paralytic, lying on his
bed; and when Jesus saw their faith he said to the
paralytic, 'Take heart, my son; your sins are forgiven.'

THE WORD IN THE PSALMS

O Lord, you will not withhold   39:12
    your compassion from me.
To you all flesh will come   64:3,4
    with its burden of sin.
If you, O Lord, should mark our guilt   129:3,4
    Lord, who would survive?
    But with you is found forgiveness:
    for this we revere you.
A humbled, contrite heart you will not spurn.   50:19

Happy those whose offence is forgiven,   31,1
    whose sin is remitted.
Lord, for the sake of your name   24:11
    forgive my guilt; for it is great.
O happy those to whom the Lord   31:2
    imputes no guilt,
    in whose spirit is no guile.
From presumption restrain your servant   18:14,13
    and let it not rule me.
But can we discern all our errors?
    From hidden faults acquit us.
Then shall I be blameless,
    clean from grave sin.

SILENT PRAYER

Jesus has entered heaven before us and on our behalf.
He, the Righteous One, is the expiation for our sins.

MEDITATION

We too as individuals, families and societies are to some
degree paralysed by sin; the spiritual vitality which is
potentially ours is withered. The first step forward is the
recognition of sinfulness in ourselves with an awareness
of our own need for forgiveness. Relying on Christ's
compassion, let us turn to the divine mercy. When we are
hurt, let us forgive that we may be forgiven.

Energy is wasted in petty rivalries and self-assertions,
in bitterness and resentment. May we remember that
when we work for others we do so for their good, not
our own self-gratification, desirous of applause and
approval. We are not star performers, but servants doing
no more than our duty.

Lord, heal us, and help us to make a definite resolve
to avoid the constant repetitions of our faults. May we
appreciate the beauty of a virtuous life.

Virtue is magnetic.

SILENT PRAYER

The Lord is all tenderness and compassion.
Lord, take pity on me a sinner.

THE WORD OF LOVE   2 Cor 5:20b,21; 6:2

We beseech you on behalf of Christ, be reconciled to God.
For our sake he made him to be sin who knew no sin, so
that in him we might become the righteousness of God.

Behold, now is the acceptable time; behold now is the
day of salvation.

He healed every infirmity

THE WORD IN THE GOSPEL   Matt 4:23,24

He went about all Galilee . . . healing every disease and
every infirmity among the people. So his fame spread
. . . and they brought him all the sick, those afflicted
with various diseases and pains, demoniacs, epileptics
and paralytics, and he healed them.

THE WORD IN THE PSALMS

Have mercy on us, Lord, have mercy.	122:4
May your love be upon us, O Lord.	32:22

He sent forth his word to heal them   106:20
   and saved their life from the grave.

It is he . . .   145:7,8
   the Lord who gives sight to the blind,
   who raises up those who are bowed down.
The Lord builds up Jerusalem;   146:2,3
   he heals the broken-hearted,
   he binds up all their wounds.
Strong is his love for us;   116:2
   he is faithful for ever.

My soul, give thanks for the Lord   102:2,3,5,10
   and never forget all his blessings.
It is he . . .
   who heals every one of your ills,
   who fills your life with good things,
   renewing your youth like an eagle's.
He does not treat us according to our sins
   nor repay us according to our faults.

SILENT PRAYER

What is lacking in Christ's suffering I will make up in my own body for the sake of the church.

MEDITATION

Like the poor, the sick are always with us, and among them are the sick in body, mind and spirit. Each yearns for healing at the deepest level, and Christ is the divine physician. Grant us, Lord, the grace of generosity with our time and energy so that we improve the quality of life of those suffering. When the house of the body is not restored to health may the house of the soul grow stronger. May we accept our own illnesses as divine gifts to be used for the salvation of others.

Prayer, a powerful strand in the healing process, is a deep reality accomplishing more than we can appreciate. Pure prayer is filled with the Spirit; the Spirit searches and refashions the very depths.

SILENT PRAYER

May all those suffering pain, illness or disease appreciate that they are chosen to be saints.

THE WORD OF LOVE   Is:61:1,2a

The Spirit of the Lord God is upon me, because the Lord has anointed me to bring good tidings to the afflicted; he has sent me to bind up the brokenhearted, to proclaim liberty to the captives, and the opening of the prison to those who are bound; to proclaim the year of the Lord's favour.

He thanked Jesus

THE WORD IN THE GOSPEL   Luke 17:14-18

As the ten lepers went they were cleansed. Then one of
them, when he saw that he was healed, turned back,
praising God with a loud voice; and he fell on his face
at Jesus' feet, giving him thanks . . . Then said Jesus, . . .
Where are the nine? Was no one found to return and
give praise to God except this foreigner?'

THE WORD IN THE PSALMS

The Lord is kind and full of compassion,   144:8,9
     slow to anger, abounding in love.
How good is the Lord to all,
     compassionate to all his creatures.

Give thanks to the Lord, all his angels,   102:20
     mighty in power, fulfiling his work,
     who heed the voice of his word.
All earth's nations and peoples,   148:11-13
     earth's leaders and rulers;
     young men and maidens,
     the old together with children.
     Let them praise the name of the Lord
     for he alone is exalted.
The splendour of his name
     reaches beyond heaven and earth.
Who in the skies can compare with the Lord   88:7
     or who is like the Lord among the children of God?

Yes, the just will praise your name;   139:13
     the upright shall live in your presence.

Alleluia!   135:1
O give thanks to the Lord for he is good,
     for his great love is without end.
Give thanks to the Lord, all his hosts,   102:21,22
     his servants who do his will.
     My soul, give thanks to the Lord!

SILENT PRAYER

What return can I make to the Lord for his gifts?
I will take the cup of salvation.

MEDITATION

Deo gratias! When we have a request to make of God
we are not slow to place it before him, and this is right,
even commendably childlike in simplicity. Yet, when
our prayer is answered in a way which corresponds to
our request – and it is important to remember we
always receive answers and coming from God they are
always excellent – do we spend a comparable time in
thanksgiving? Do we thank the Lord for all his
answers?

An expression of thanks and appreciation not merely
avoids taking someone else for granted, but builds up
the other person. Let us give thanks for Christian values
in homes and schools, health in mind and body,
generous friends and supportive neighbours . . . Deo
gratias!

SILENT PRAYER

God is supremely generous!
Let us sing in our hearts and give thanks for
everything.

THE WORD OF LOVE   Tobit 12:6

Praise God and give thanks to him; exalt him and give
thanks to him in the presence of all the living for what
he has done for you. It is good to praise God and to
exalt his name, worthily declaring the works of God. Do
not be slow to give him thanks.

'He who humbles himself will be exalted'

The Word In The Gospel

Luke 14:11

'Everyone who exalts himself will be humbled, and he who humbles himself will be exalted.'

The Word In The Psalms

Neither from the east nor from the west, 74:7,8
    nor from the desert or mountains comes judgment,
    but God himself is the judge.
One he humbles, another he exalts.
He guides the humble in the right path; 24:9
    he teaches his way to the poor.

The Lord is great and almighty; 146:5,6,11
    his wisdom can never be measured.
The Lord raises the lowly;
    he humbles the wicked to the dust.
The Lord delights in those who revere him,
    in those who wait for his love.
The Lord supports all who fall 114:14,18
    and he raises all who are bowed down.
He is close to all who call him,
    who call on him from their hearts.
From the dust he lifts up the lowly, 112:7,8
    from the dungheap he raises the poor
    to set them in the company of rulers,
    yes, with the rulers of his people.

Alleluia! 150:1,2,6
Praise God in his holy place,
    praise his surpassing greatness.
Let everything that lives and that breathes
    give praise to the Lord. Alleluia!

SILENT PRAYER

> Let us keep the fear of God before the eyes of the
> soul.
> It is at all times a first step towards humility.

MEDITATION

Pride is so persistent a nuisance that even from childhood
we need to learn that there is nothing more sublime than
humility. As union with truth constitutes humility, it is
not incompatible with both praise and encouragement
which are honest and justified. We must distinguish
between the counterfeit and the genuine. Authentic
study, a delight in itself, is not to be confused with a rat-
race for paper qualifications; it can lead us to growth in
humility and thus in holiness.

Almighty Lord, help us to be realistic and recognise
our debilitating weaknesses and your infinite wisdom.
From such a position may we live and grow in love of
you and of others.

SILENT PRAYER

> Only if we are humble of heart may our lives on earth
> be raised to the spiritual heights.

THE WORD OF LOVE   Rom 11:33-36

O depth of the riches and wisdom and knowledge of
God! How unsearchable are his judgments and how
inscrutable his ways!
'For who has known the mind of the Lord,
   or who has been his counsellor?
Or who has given a gift to him
   that he might be repaid?'
For from him and through him and to him are all things.
To him be glory for ever. Amen.

Receive the kingdom like a child

THE WORD IN THE GOSPEL

Mark 10:15

'Truly, I say to you, whoever does not receive the kingdom of God like a child shall not enter it.'

THE WORD IN THE PSALMS

The rule of the Lord is to be trusted, 18:8
    it gives wisdom to the simple.

O Lord, . . . 130:1,2
I have not gone after things too great
    nor marvels beyond me.
Truly I have set my soul
    in silence and peace.
A weaned child on its mother's breasts,
    even so is my soul.
Your majesty is praised above the heavens; 8:2,3
    on the lips of children and of babes
    you have found praise to foil your enemy,
    to silence the foe and the rebel.
The helpless trusts himself to you; 9:10,14
    for you are the helper of the orphan.

Surely goodness and kindness shall follow me 22:6
    all the days of my life.
And my soul shall live for him,
    my children serve him. 21:30-32
They shall tell of the Lord to generations yet to come,
    declare his faithfulness to peoples yet unborn:
    'These things the Lord has done.'

SILENT PRAYER

Help me, Lord, to absorb the lesson taught by any 'little one' of yours.

MEDITATION

'Will your teacher know the answer?'

'Yes,' replied the five year old, 'teachers know everything.'

The grown-up smiled; the issue had been settled decisively. Furthermore, the small child, accepting us as we are, seeks only our love and attention.

Christ, the rising sun, bestows on each of us, rays of tender care to fill us with his plenitude. Of his fullness we are all receiving, grace upon grace. It is holy to be simple; and that is hard, but not complicated.

Father, may we develop the trustful simplicity of the child to cut through sophisticated complexities and recognise that we have but one teacher, Christ the Lord; he truly knows the answer before we have so much as articulated the question surfacing in sometimes critical or grumbling hearts.

SILENT PRAYER

Do not despise one of these little ones; in heaven their angels always behold the face of my Father.

THE WORD OF LOVE   1 John 3:1a,2

See what love the Father has given us, that we should be called children of God; and so we are . . . Beloved, we are God's children now; it does not yet appear what we shall be, but we know that when he appears we shall be like him, for we shall see him as he is.

'I am the living bread'

The Word In The Gospel

John 6:49,51

Your ancestors ate the manna in the wilderness, and
they died . . . I am the living bread that came down
from heaven. Whoever eats of this bread will live
forever; and the bread that I will give for the life of the
world is my flesh.

The Word In The Psalms

Preserve me, God, I take refuge in you.   15:1

Taste and see that the Lord is good.   33:9
They are happy who seek refuge in him.
Mere mortals ate the bread of angels.   77:25
He sent them abundance of food.
He filled them with bread from heaven.   104:40
He rained down manna for their food,   77:24
    and gave them bread from heaven.

Revere the Lord, you his saints.   33:10,11
They lack nothing, those who revere him.
Strong lions suffer want and go hungry
    but those who seek the Lord lack no blessing.
Pay your sacrifice of thanksgiving to God   49:14
    and render him your votive offerings.
It is he who keep faith for ever;   145:6,7
    it is he who gives bread to the hungry.
He gives food to those who fear him;   110:5
    keeps his covenant ever in mind.
Whoever is wise, let him heed these things   106:43
    and consider the love of the Lord

I will walk in the presence of the Lord   114:9
    in the land of the living.
Let me sing to the Lord for his goodness to me,   12:7
    singing psalms to the name of the Lord, the Most High.

76

SILENT PRAYER

May all be one as you are, Father, in me and I in you.

MEDITATION

Through our participation in the Eucharist, the body and blood of Christ, we become what we receive. We renew our offering of our very selves to God and do so in the specific circumstances of our daily lives. As we worship God we are sanctified; as we are sanctified the Mystical Body of Christ is built up. His power is made perfect in weakness. Lord, may we contemplate unceasingly the gift we have received and may we produce the fruit of greater love.

We intercede for the unity of the parish community which is made manifest in the worthy celebration of the Eucharist. May disagreements and jealousies be discarded. Lord, we thank you for the living bread which bestows on us so powerful a pledge of eternal happiness.

SILENT PRAYER

The kingdom of God is very close to us.
O hidden Lord, enrich us with your grace.

THE WORD OF LOVE   1 Cor 11:23b-25

The Lord Jesus on the night when he was betrayed took bread, and when he had given thanks he broke it, and said, 'This is my body which is for you. Do this in remembrance of me.' In the same way also the cup, after supper, saying, 'This cup is the new covenant in my blood. Do this, as often as you drink it, in remembrance of me.'

'I am the light of the world'

John 8:12

THE WORD IN THE GOSPEL

'I am the light of the world. Whoever follows me will
never walk in darkness, but will have the light of life.'

THE WORD IN THE PSALMS

Some lay in darkness and in gloom . . .   106:10,13-15
Then they cried to the Lord in their need
   and he rescued them from their distress.
He led them forth from darkness and gloom:
   let them thank the Lord for his goodness,
   for the wonders he does for his people.

Light shines forth for the just;   96:11,12
   and joy for the upright of heart.
Rejoice, you just, in the Lord;
   give glory to his holy name.

O Lord, you search me and you know me,   138:1,3,11,12
   all my ways lie open to you.
If I say: 'Let the darkness hide me
   and the light around me be night,'
   even darkness is not dark for you
   and the night is as clear as the day.
The Lord is my light and my help;   26:1
   whom shall I fear?
He is a light in the darkness for the upright: 111:4
   he is generous, merciful and just.
The command of the Lord is clear,   18:9
   it gives light to the eyes.
Bless the Lord, my soul!   103:1,2
Lord God, how great you are,
   clothed in majesty and glory,
   wrapped in light as in a robe!

SILENT PRAYER

Lord, may we be radiant with your supernatural
splendour.
May we carry your light to others.

MEDITATION

No matter how stunning our personal, local, national or
international suffering may be at any particular
moment, we must eventually and in the final analysis
come out of the darkness to the person of the risen
Christ. Equally, no matter how dazzling our joy and
success, we will be seeing it only in a gaudy glare if we
do not refer it back to Christ, the Light of the first Easter
Sunday. All our disappointments, our aspirations and
our personal relationships can be lived in true focus
only if we allow him to illumine them.

Lord, we give thanks for those who, hour by hour,
radiate the light of Christ into a world numbed by
seemingly meaningless suffering and blinded by
superficially glittering distractions. Increase our faith
that we may see the more clearly.

SILENT PRAYER

Lord, help us to discern how the noblest deeds are
illumined by rays of forgiveness, patience and
generosity.

THE WORD OF LOVE   Col 1:11-14

May you be strengthened with all power, according to
his glorious might, giving thanks to the Father, who has
qualified us to share in the inheritance of the saints in
light. He has delivered us from the dominion of
darkness and transferred us to the kingdom of his
beloved Son, in whom we have redemption, the
forgiveness of sins.

'I am the resurrection
and the life'

The Word In The Gospel   John 11:25,26

'I am the resurrection and the life. Those who believe in
me, even though they die, will live, and everyone who
lives and believes in me shall never die.'

The Word In The Psalms

The heavens proclaim the glory of God,   18:2,5-7
   and the firmament shows forth the work of his hands.
There he has placed a tent for the sun;
    it comes forth like a bridegroom coming from his tent,
    rejoices like a champion to run its course.
At the end of the sky is the rising of the sun;
   to the furthest end of the sky is its course.
    There is nothing concealed from its burning heat.

Commit your life to the Lord,   36:5,6
   trust in him and he will act,
    so that your justice breaks forth like the light,
    your cause like the noon-day sun.
Happy those who consider the poor and the weak.   40:2,3
   The Lord will save them in the day of evil,
   will guard them, give them life, make them
   happy in the land
   and will not give them up to the will of their foes.

To you, Lord, I cried,   29:9-11
   to my God I made appeal:
   'What profit would my death be, my going to the
grave?
   Can dust give you praise or proclaim your truth?'
The Lord listened and had pity.
   The Lord came to my help.
I will praise you, Lord my God, with all my heart   85:12,13

and glorify your name for ever;
for your love to me has been great:
you have saved me from the depths of the grave.

SILENT PRAYER

I have risen; I am still with you.
O Lord, you are the Christ, the Son of God.

MEDITATION

The liturgical year of the church revolves around the
Paschal Mystery; Christ is risen. Is my own personal
spiritual life similarly centred on and rooted in his
Resurrection? If not, how can I bring it into focus?

Lord, grant us the grace to think deeply with our
minds in our hearts. It is no soft option, but demands hard
labour and time. Is it worthwhile? How shallow the
question since what is at stake is the fullness of life,
nothing less than sharing in the divine life!

Let us praise God with our lives since Christ, the rising
sun, is raising us to that eternal life into which we were
born at our baptism. May we help others to live the
Paschal Mystery by giving them the affirmation,
recognition and healing for which they long.

SILENT PRAYER

Life's own champion, slain, yet lives to reign.
To him be glory and power for ever!

THE WORD OF LOVE   Rom 14:7-9

None of us lives to himself, and none of us dies to
himself. If we live, we live to the Lord and if we die, we
die to the Lord; so then, whether we live or whether we
die, we are the Lord's. For this end Christ died and lived
again, that he might be Lord both of the dead and of the
living.

'I am the way and the truth and the life'

THE WORD IN THE GOSPEL

Jesus said to him, 'I am the way, and the truth, and the life; no one comes to the Father, but by me.'

THE WORD IN THE PSALMS

O blessed are those who fear the Lord   127:1
  and walk in his ways!
Let the praise of God be on their lips   149:6,9
    and a two-edged sword in their hand,
    to carry out the sentence pre-ordained:
    this honour is for all his faithful.
The Lord guards the way of the just.   1:6

Examine me, Lord, and try me;   25:2-4
    O test my heart and my mind,
    for your love is before my eyes
    and I walk according to your truth.
I never take my place with liars
    and with hypocrites I shall not go.
Lord, make me know your ways.   24:4,5
    Lord, teach me your paths.
    Make me walk in your truth, and teach me,
    for you are God my saviour.
O search me, God, and know my heart.   138:23,24
    O test me and know my thoughts.
    See that I follow not the wrong path,
    and lead me in the path of life eternal.
My heart rejoices, my soul is glad.   15:9,11
You will show me the path of life,
    the fullness of joy in your presence,
    at your right hand happiness for ever.

SILENT PRAYER

Lord, show me the way to the Father.
Keep me true to your teaching; never let me be parted
from you.

MEDITATION

If our lives are to be centred on Christ, we must walk in
his way and in his truth. The love of Christ must be our
priority. To live well, to pray well and to think well will
enhance our vision of truth. Lord, we acknowledge that
we are called to adhere to moral truth; grant us the grace
to live out whatever demands this may make of us.

Truth demands a total gift of ourselves, and he who is
Truth gives a total gift of himself. We rejoice in our
personal freedom which enables us to respond and
experience the liberating force of divine love. Lord, we
recognise the universal and permanent validity of divine
revelation. Help us to appreciate the beauty of truth.

SILENT PRAYER

Lord, by your cross and resurrection you have set me
free.
How am I living that glorious freedom?

THE WORD OF LOVE   Eph 1:16-20a

I do not cease to give thanks for you, remembering you in
my prayers, that the God of our Lord Jesus Christ, the
Father of glory, may give you a spirit of wisdom and of
revelation in the knowledge of him, having the eyes of
your hearts enlightened, that you may know what is the
hope to which he has called you, what are the riches of
his glorious inheritance in the saints, and what is the
immeasurable greatness of his power in us who believe,
according to the working of his great might which he
accomplished in Christ.

'Love one another'

THE WORD IN THE GOSPEL
John 13:34

'A new commandment I give to you, that you love one another; even as I have loved you, that you also love one another.'

THE WORD IN THE PSALMS

The words of the Lord are words without alloy,	11:7

The words of the Lord are words without alloy,   11:7
   silver from the furnace, seven times refined.
Good people take pity and lend,   111:5,9
   they conduct their affairs with honour.
Open-handed, they give to the poor;
   their justice stands firm for ever.
Their heads will be raised in glory.

How good and how pleasant it is,   132:1,3
   when people live in unity!
It is like the dew of Hermon which falls
   on the heights of Zion.
For there the Lord gives his blessing,
   life for ever.

Not to us, Lord, not to us,   113:1
   but to your name give the glory
   for the sake of your love and your truth.
The Lord of hosts is with us: 45:8
   the God of Jacob is our stronghold.
The law of the Lord is perfect.   18:8

I will sing for ever of your love, O Lord;   88:2,3
   through all ages my mouth will proclaim your truth.
Of this I am sure, that your love lasts for ever,
   that your truth is firmly established as the heavens.
Your love, Lord, reaches to heaven;   35:6
   your truth to the skies.

Silent Prayer

May our love be faithful and tender, rooted in the
words of Christ.

Meditation

The new commandment has revolutionary implications
for human relationships. Loving a friend sounds easy,
but true love, consisting of loving our friend in God,
has a different perspective, one far removed from self.
The 'difficult personality' in the family, workplace or
community, the one who is aloof or gushing, arrogant
or cunning, is to be loved for the sake of God. That
challenges us all our days. Christ is demanding that we
behave as he behaves. Nothing less than daily
meditation in which we stoke up the furnace of our
hearts, will enkindle the divine love within us and give
us the strength we do not have of ourselves.

Lord, when we fall as fall we will, grant us the grace
to stand up and start all over again and again . . .

Silent Prayer

Lord, bless those who are 'difficult'!
May we patiently support the weaknesses of others,
even those most irritating.

The Word Of Love   1 Cor 13:4-7

Love is patient and kind; love is not jealous or boastful;
it is not arrogant or rude. Love does not insist on its
own way; it is not irritable or resentful; it does not
rejoice at wrong, but rejoices in the right. Love bears all
things, believes all things, hopes all things, endures all
things.

'There was a great earthquake'

THE WORD IN THE GOSPEL   Matt 28:1,2

Now after the sabbath, toward the dawn of the first day
of the week, Mary Magdalene and the other Mary went
to see the sepulchre. And behold, there was a great
earthquake.

THE WORD IN THE PSALMS

The waves of death rose about me;	17:5-7
the snares of the grave entangled me.	
I cried to my God for help:	
Arise, O God, and defend your cause!	73:22
Arise, Lord, let men not prevail!	9:20
O Lord, do not leave me alone,	21:20
my strength, make haste to help me!	
My cry came to his ears.	17:7

Then the earth reeled and rocked.   17:8,16
The bed of the ocean was revealed;
    the foundations of the world were laid bare
    at the thunder of your threat, O Lord,
    at the blast of the breath of your anger.
Tremble, O earth, before the Lord,   113:7
    in the presence of the God of Jacob.
A fire prepares his path;   96:3,4
    it burns up his foes on every side.
His lightnings light up the world,
    the earth trembles at the sight.

You, Lord, are a shield about me,   3:4
    my glory, who lift up my head.
So my soul sings psalms to you unceasingly.   29:13
O Lord my God, I will thank you for ever.

SILENT PRAYER

> This is the day which the Lord has made.
> Let us rejoice and be glad.

MEDITATION

One great and terrible Friday a story seemed to have ended. It had not. On occasion our own world seems destroyed and we call on the Lord's name, the only one by which we can be saved. Our cry comes to his ears; he knows everything including the future. A shattering event essentially foreshadows the rising to a new life built on more penetrating spiritual insights.

The earth trembles. The underworld is open and surrenders the dead; heaven's gate is open and the dead are welcomed. Let us rejoice that we are thought worthy of forgiveness.

O risen Lord, we renew our trust in you. You understand our all too human insecurity and our spiritual potential. May we be utterly convinced that in these latter days the whole of creation is tending upwards.

SILENT PRAYER

> The Lord is our strength! He is raising us upwards.
> May we become one body, one spirit in Christ.

THE WORD OF LOVE   Col 2:9,10a,12

For in him the whole fullness of deity dwells bodily, and you have come to fullness of life in him . . . You were buried with him in baptism, in which you were also raised with him, through faith in the working of God, who raised him from the dead.

The stone was rolled back

THE WORD IN THE GOSPEL

Matt 28:2

An angel of the Lord descended from heaven and came
and rolled back the stone, and sat upon it.

THE WORD IN THE PSALMS

Your love, O Lord, is eternal,   137:7
    discard not the work of your hands.
Display your great love, you whose right hand saves. 16:7
With you I can break through any barrier.   17:30

From on high he reached down and seized me; 17:17,18,20
    he snatched me from my powerful foe.
He brought me forth into freedom,
    he saved me because he loved me.
It is better to take refuge in the Lord   117:8
    than to trust in mortals.
The angel of the Lord is encamped   33:8
    around those who revere him to rescue them.

Alleluia!   114:1
I love the Lord for he has heard
    the cry of my appeal.
I was thrust down, thrust down and falling 117:13,14
    but the Lord was my helper.
    The Lord is my strength and my song;
    he was my saviour.
I thank you, Lord, with all my heart,   137:1-3
    you have heard the words of my mouth.
Before the angels I will bless you.
    I will adore before your holy temple.
    On the day I called, you answered.

SILENT PRAYER

> May your good spirit guide me to break through any
> barrier.

MEDITATION

A variety of obstacles, some erected by people over
many centuries, divide us from one another. Class
distinctions, racial and religious prejudices are among
them. Yet, these heavy stones in society can be rolled
back. However, our assent is essential for God has
graciously given us free will. Indeed it is of the very
essence of our human nature and, though much
mutilated by original sin, it can be strengthened and
refined by prayer.

Lord, grant us real courage to face the clutter, the
debris and the barriers within us, caused so often by
inherited attitudes. May we have the strength and
patience to build lighter spiritual dwellings with
windows looking out to panoramic views of a new
heaven and a new earth.

SILENT PRAYER

> Pluck out the granite of prejudice;
> replace it with the jewel of compassion.

THE WORD OF LOVE   1 Pet 2:4-5

Come to him, a living stone, though rejected by mortals
yet chosen and precious in God's sight; and like living
stones let yourselves be built into a spiritual house, to
be a holy priesthood, to offer spiritual sacrifices
acceptable to God through Jesus Christ.

The guards became like dead men

THE WORD IN THE GOSPEL   Matt 28:3,4

The angel's appearance was like lightning, and his raiment white as snow. And for fear of him the guards trembled and became like dead men.

THE WORD IN THE PSALMS

I love you, Lord, my strength.   17:1

From your temple you heard my voice.   17:7,10-14
You lowered the heavens and came down,
    a black cloud under your feet.
You came enthroned on the cherubim,
    you flew on the wings of the wind.
You made the darkness your covering,
    the dark waters of the clouds, your tent.
A brightness shone out before you
    with hailstones and flashes of fire.
Lord you thundered in the heavens;
    Most High, you let your voice be heard.
You set up your tent in Jerusalem.   75:3,4,6
    It was there you broke the flashing arrows,
    the shield, the sword, the armour.
The warriors, despoiled, slept in death;
    the hands of the soldiers were powerless.

Your servant, Lord, your servant am I;   115:16
you have loosened my bonds.

You shot your arrows, scattered the foe,   17:15,51
    flashed your lightnings, and put them to flight.
You have given great victories to your king
    and shown your love for your anointed,
    for David and his line for ever.
From Zion may the Lord be blessed,   134:21
    he who dwells in Jerusalem!

SILENT PRAYER

Let us not lose our nerve; let us recognise that the victory is ours. Christ is risen!

MEDITATION

The dead man was, or so they said, only a carpenter's son, and the power of the Roman Empire had been ranged against him. It seemed scarcely a contest. Yet, on the third day, a day of serenity and splendour, Christ rose from the dead. Christian communities grew spontaneously; the power of the State could not withstand them. Lord, we pray for all holding secular authority that they may use their power wisely and that we may be able to live peaceful spiritual lives.

St. Antony of Egypt advised: 'Let Christ be your life's breath, and place your confidence in him.' There indeed is the true depth and meaning of our lives as Christians. May we witness the growth of the Mystical Body of Christ in our world.

SILENT PRAYER

We are confident we shall see the Lord's victory on our behalf.

THE WORD OF LOVE   1 Cor 15:20-22

Christ has been raised from the dead, the first fruits of those who have fallen asleep. For as by a man came death, by a man has come also the resurrection of the dead. For as in Adam all die, so also in Christ shall all be made alive.

Do not be afraid: he is risen

Matt 28:5,6

THE WORD IN THE GOSPEL

The angel said to the women, 'Do not be afraid; for I
know that you seek Jesus who was crucified. He is not
here; for he has risen, as he said.'

THE WORD IN THE PSALMS

Raise a song and sound the timbrel,   80:3,4
    the sweet-sounding harp and the lute,
    blow the trumpet at the new moon,
    when the moon is full on our feast.

The nations all encompassed me;   117:10-12,39,43,38
    in the Lord's name I crushed them.
They compassed me, compassed me about;
    in the Lord's name I crushed them.
They compassed me about like bees;
    they blazed like a fire among thorns.
    In the Lord's name I crushed them.
I smote them so they could not rise;   17:39,43,38
    they fell beneath my feet.
I crushed them fine as dust before the wind;
    trod them down like dirt in the streets.
I pursued and overtook my foes,
    never turning back till they were slain.

My heart is ready, O God;   107:2,3
    I will sing, sing your praise.
Awake, my soul;
    awake, lyre and harp.
I will awake the dawn.
Come and hear, all who fear God.   65:16
    I will tell what he did for my soul.

SILENT PRAYER

The Almighty works marvels for us.
Christ is our ransom and our salvation.

MEDITATION

Fear paralyses. Do not be afraid! The angels words
speak to us of a life-giving reality, the triumph of Christ
over the dominion of darkness; in today's world heroic
commitment may sometimes be needed if we are to be
Christ's disciples. It is God's will that we should bear
'the image of the man of heaven'. May we set ourselves
close to the risen Lord; may he bless our current
projects and enterprises.

Lord, Jesus, deepen our understanding of the
liberating force of divine love and help us to proclaim
your Resurrection to an apathetic and cynical world.

May we progress from glory to glory in Christ Jesus
our Lord.

SILENT PRAYER

Christ is truly risen.
He is the light of his people, whom he has redeemed
with his blood.

THE WORD OF LOVE   Col 3:3,4,12

You have died, and your life is hid with Christ in God.
When Christ who is our life appears, then you also will
appear with him in glory. Put on then, as God's chosen
ones, holy and beloved, compassion, kindness,
lowliness, meekness and patience.

'I have seen the Lord'

THE WORD IN THE GOSPEL   John 20:18

Mary Magdalene went and said to the disciples, 'I have
seen the Lord.'

THE WORD IN THE PSALMS

Alleluia!   112:1,3
Praise, O servants of the Lord,
    praise the name of the Lord!
From the rising of the sun to its setting
    praised be the name of the Lord!
This day was made by the Lord;   117:24,15,16
    we rejoice and are glad.
The Lord's right hand has triumphed;
    his right hand raised me.
The Lord's right hand has triumphed.
It is good to give thanks to the Lord,   91:2-4
    to make music to your name, O Most High,
    to proclaim your love in the morning,
    on the ten-stringed lyre and the lute.
The Lord is great, highly to be praised,   144:3
    his greatness cannot be measured.

My heart is ready, O God,   56:8,9
    my heart is ready.
    I will sing, I will sing your praise.
Awake my soul;
    awake lyre and harp,
    I will awake the dawn.
For you have rescued me from all my distress   53:9
    and my eyes have seen the downfall of my foes.
He is happy who is helped by Jacob's God,   145:5
    whose hope is in the Lord his God.

94

Silent Prayer

Christ, my hope, has risen.
The immeasurable riches of his grace are open to me.

Meditation

Mary Magdelene, who persevered in seeking Christ,
found him. May we follow in her footsteps.

An encounter with the risen Christ, the dynamic
source of a new life, will always convey to us an inner
certainty of its reality. Redemption's day has dawned.
What previously were life's scales of values have been
turned topsy-turvy. The challenge before us is to
preserve the vision of God's love for us in Christ and to
keep on deriving new results from this encounter.
Which areas of my life must change if I am to become
more like Christ?

Lord, grant us the grace to change our feelings,
outlook and behaviour so that we may truly become the
people of God, and not of the world. Let us not be
disheartened since the work of grace is a slow work.

Silent Prayer

May I seek him whom my soul loves.
O Christ, take possession of me at every level of my
life.

The Word Of Love   Eph 2:4-7

God, who is rich in mercy, out of the great love with
which he loved us, even when we were dead through
our trespasses, made us alive together with Christ and
raised us up with him, and made us sit with him in the
heavenly places in Christ Jesus, that in the coming ages
he might show the immeasurable riches of his grace in
kindness towards us in Christ Jesus.

The disciples were glad

THE WORD IN THE GOSPEL   John 20:20

Jesus showed them his hands and his side. Then the disciples were glad.

THE WORD IN THE PSALMS

I sought the Lord and he answered me;   33:5
    from all my terrors he set me free.
I will sing to the Lord all my life,   103:33
    make music to my God while I live.

The Lord is king, with majesty enrobed;   92:1
    the Lord has robed himself with might,
    he has girded himself with power.
Serve the Lord with gladness.   99:2
    Come before him, singing for joy.

Alleluia!   149:1
Sing a new song to the Lord,
    his praise in the assembly of the faithful.
Give thanks to the Lord upon the harp,   32:2,3
    with a ten-stringed lute sing him songs.
O sing him a song that is new,
    play loudly, with all your skill.
O praise him with resounding cymbals,   150:5,4
    praise him with clashing of cymbals;
    praise him with strings and pipes.
Let Zion's people exult in their king.   149:2,3
Let them praise his name with dancing
    and make music with timbrel and harp.
The Lord will reign for ever,   145:10
    Zion's God, from age to age.

SILENT PRAYER

O Lord, come and make your abode with us.
May we sing to you with our lives.

MEDITATION

Behold the God-man; indeed the disciples were glad! Christ the Lord is truly risen, his wounds still visible. In him we find healing for the whole person, spirit, soul and body. Let us rejoice in the deep recesses of our souls and be open to Christ transforming our mediation into a melodious harmony if he so wills. With our gaze fixed on the risen Christ our souls may sing a canticle of love and praise. Regardless of those things which could depress our spirits, let us praise him in a spiritual song.

Lord, we also thank you for the gift of music which has enriched liturgical celebrations over the centuries and for those composers and performers whose excellence gives expression to our supernatural joy.

SILENT PRAYER

My heart rejoices in the risen Christ.
May my life always bear witness to his kingship.

THE WORD OF LOVE   Acts 13:30-33a

God raised him from the dead; and for many days he appeared to those who came up with him from Galilee to Jerusalem, who are now his witnesses to the people. And we bring you the good news that what God promised to the fathers, this he has fulfilled to us their children by raising Jesus.

'He opened to us the scriptures'

THE WORD IN THE GOSPEL   Luke 24:27,32

Beginning with Moses and all the prophets, he interpreted to them in all the scriptures the things concerning himself . . . They said to each other, 'Did not our hearts burn within us while he talked to us on the road, while he opened to us the scriptures?'

THE WORD IN THE PSALMS

Who can tell the Lord's mighty deeds?	105:2
Who can recount all his praise?	

Glorify the Lord with me.	33:4
Together let us praise his name.	
They surrounded me, the snares of death,	114:3
with the anguish of the tomb;	
they caught me, sorrow and distress.	
When the poor cry out the Lord hears them	33:7
and rescues them from all their distress.	
He rewarded me because I was just,	17:21,22
repaid me, for my hands were clean,	
for I have kept the way of the Lord	
and have not fallen away from my God.	
The Lord ransoms the souls of his servants.	33:23,6
Those who hide in him shall not be condemned.	
Look towards him and be radiant;	
let your faces not be abashed.	
The Lord gives the word to the bearers	
of good tidings:	67:12
'The Almighty has defeated a numberless army . . .'	
See how the evil-doers fall!	35:13
Flung down, they shall never arise.	

Let me speak the praise of the Lord,	144:21
let all peoples bless your holy name	
for ever, for ages unending.	

SILENT PRAYER

The word of God is alive and active, sharper than any two-edged sword, piercing to the division of soul and spirit.

MEDITATION

The two disciples at Emmaus were glad. Each day their joy may be ours because the Bible is indeed a true guide for human life. The word of God is revealed to us in the scriptures. The words are not to be read at speed or skimmed on the surface, both practical devices in a world inundated with the products of word-processors. They are rather to be absorbed into the depths of our personalities. In the quest for increasing enlightenment we can compare verses in one text with those in another, eventually moving around the Bible with the ease of one at home.

Grant us, Lord, the grace to set time aside for slow meditative scripture reading. May we appreciate that this is not the work of the analytical mind, but of the listening heart.

SILENT PRAYER

The power of God is in his word.
May neither sloth nor apathy blunt his word; may it penetrate the depths of my being.

THE WORD OF LOVE   Rev 15:3,4

They sing the song of Moses, the servant of God, and the song of the Lamb, saying,
'Great and wonderful are thy deeds,
O Lord God the Almighty!
Just and true are thy ways,
O king of the ages!
Who shall not fear and glorify thy name, O Lord?
For thou alone art holy.
All nations shall come and worship thee,
for thy judgments have been revealed.'

They recognised him in the breaking of bread

THE WORD IN THE GOSPEL   Luke 24:30,31

When he was at table with them, he took the bread and
blessed and broke it, and gave it to them. And their
eyes were opened and they recognised him.

THE WORD IN THE PSALMS

The Lord has sworn an oath he will not change.   109:4
    'You are a priest for ever,
    a priest like Melchizedech of old.'
He has sent deliverance to his people   110:9,10
    and established his covenant for ever.
    Holy his name, to be feared.
His praise shall last for ever!

You have prepared a banquet for me.   22:5
The cup of salvation I will raise.   115:13
My head you have anointed with oil;   22:5
    my cup is overflowing.
A sacrifice of thanks giving honours me   49:23
    and I will show God's salvation to the upright.
Let there be rejoicing and gladness   69:5
    for all who seek you.

How lovely is your dwelling place,   83:2,5,11
    Lord, God of hosts.
They are happy who dwell in your house,
    for ever singing your praise.
One day within your courts
    is better than a thousand elsewhere.
O praise the Lord, Jerusalem!   147:12,14
    Zion, praise your God!
He established peace on your borders,
    he feeds you with finest wheat.

SILENT PRAYER

> May we seek the spiritual insight which recognises
> Christ the High Priest, the one always able to save us.

MEDITATION

Christ abides in us and we in him. As we recall the mysteries of our redemption, help us Lord to meditate more profoundly on the Eucharistic sacrifice as both the source and summit of the church's worship and of the Christian life. May the outward signs used become more intelligible, penetrating our minds and hearts in ever greater depth. We pray for all preparing to receive the sacraments that they may live the faith they profess.

In a world of social, economic and political tension we are called to be ambassadors of Christ, the Prince of Peace. The task is daunting, demanding more strength than we possess; our eyes must be open to his presence which alone can nourish and sustain us.

SILENT PRAYER

> Yet a little while and the coming one shall come.
> O Lord, draw us closer to you and to one another.

THE WORD OF LOVE   Jer 31:11,12a,14

The Lord has ransomed Jacob,
   and has redeemed him from hands too strong for him.
They shall come and sing aloud on the height of Zion,
   and they shall be radiant over the goodness of the
Lord,
   over the grain, the wine and the oil . . .
I will feast the soul of the priests with abundance,
   and my people shall be satisfied with my goodness,
says the Lord.

The eleven had not believed

THE WORD IN THE GOSPEL   Mark 16:14

Jesus appeared to the eleven themselves as they sat at table; and he upbraided them for their unbelief and hardness of heart, because they had not believed those who saw him after he had risen.

THE WORD IN THE PSALMS

You rebels, how long will your hearts be closed,   4:3
    will you love what is futile and seek what is false?

Those who put their trust in the Lord   124:1
    are like Mount Zion, that cannot be shaken,
    that stands for ever.
I have said: 'You call yourselves gods   81:6
    and all of you, children of the Most High.'
This God of ours is a God who saves.   67:21
The Lord our God holds the keys of death.

Around me the just will assemble   141:8
    because of your goodness to me.
I will praise you, Lord, you have rescued me   29:2-4
    and have not let my enemies rejoice over me.
O Lord, I cried to you for help
    and you, my God, have healed me.
O Lord, you have raised my soul from the dead,
    restored me to life from those who sink into the grave.
I will tell of your name to my brethren   21:23
    and will praise you where they are assembled.
Seven times a day I praise you   118:164
    for your just decrees.

O Lord, how great are your works!   91:6
    How deep are your designs!

SILENT PRAYER

Open your heart to the glory of the risen Christ.
Ponder the wondrous meaning of his resurrection.

MEDITATION

Our true potential can be smothered by the dulling
cover of self-satisfaction or timidity, and yet, living in
an age of scepticism, the world desperately needs our
glorious message that Christ is truly risen. Let us
simply cling in faith to this central wonder of our
redemption; this will make all other issues more
amenable to being viewed and handled from a new
perspective. May our spiritual sight be trained to
recognise the risen Christ, to communicate him to
others and thus to convert the world.

Lord, help us to expel the darkness of doubt from
our minds and to reply with gentle clarity to those who
challenge our faith. May we remember that we share in
the divinity of Christ.

SILENT PRAYER

Lord, increase our faith and our joy.
Christ our king is victorious!

THE WORD OF LOVE   1 Pet 1:8,9

Without having seen him you love him; though you do
not now see him you believe in him and rejoice with
unutterable and exalted joy. As the outcome of your
faith you obtain the salvation of your souls.

'Peace be with you'

THE WORD IN THE GOSPEL   John 20:26

Eight days later, his disciples were again in the house,
and Thomas was with them. The doors were shut, but
Jesus came and stood among them, and said, 'Peace be
with you.'

THE WORD IN THE PSALMS

For love of my family and friends   121:8
    I say: 'Peace upon you!'

Come, children, and hear me   33:12-15
    that I may teach you the fear of the Lord.
Who are those who long for life?
Then keep your tongue from evil
    and your lips from speaking deceit.
Turn aside from evil and do good;
    seek and strive after peace.
I will never take back my love;   88:34
    my truth will never fail.
For the peace of Jerusalem pray: 121:6,7
    'Peace be to your homes!
    May peace reign in your walls,
    in your palaces, peace!'
The Lord tests the just and the wicked: 10:5
    the lover of violence he hates.

The Lord who is just has destroyed   128:4
    the yoke of the wicked.

Let there be joy for those who love my cause.   34:27
Let them say without end:
    'Great is the Lord who delights
    in the peace of his servant.'
On Israel, peace!   124:5

Silent Prayer

Lamb of God, Redeemer of the world, grant us peace.
Those who trust in you live in perfect peace.

Meditation

Christ's greeting, 'Peace be with you', had been
wondrously foreshadowed at his birth by the multitude
of the heavenly host declaring 'Peace to all people who
are God's friends'. The King of Peace was standing in a
locked upper room full of frightened people, and his
presence gave them new strength. O risen Christ, you
are our peace and strength.

Our yearning for true peace sets us apart from the
world and unites us to each other and to God. Lord,
may our sensitivity to peace be increased by taking a
keener delight in your manifold gifts, a day of rest, the
dawn chorus, the many shades of colour in a garden, a
beautiful sunset, a starry night. Let us remember that
when God made man and woman he placed them in a
garden.

Silent Prayer

May our presence bring the peace of Christ to those
whom we meet.

The Word Of Love   1 John 1:1,2

That which was from the beginning, which we have
heard, which we have seen with our eyes, which we
have looked upon and touched with our hands,
concerning the word of life – the life was made
manifest, and we saw it, and testify to it, and proclaim
to you the eternal life which was with the Father and
was made manifest to us.

'My Lord and my God'

THE WORD IN THE GOSPEL   John 20:27,28

Then Jesus said to Thomas, 'Put your finger here, and
see my hands; and put out your hand, and place it in
my side; do not be faithless, but believing.' Thomas
answered him, 'My Lord and my God!'

THE WORD IN THE PSALMS

For who is God but you, Lord?   17:32
Who is a rock but you, my God?

I say to the Lord: 'You are my God.   15:2
  My happiness lies in you alone.'
You are my God, I thank you.   117:28
  My God, I praise you.
Let my prayer arise before you like incense,   140:2
  the raising of my hands like an evening oblation.

The stone which the builders rejected   117:22,23
  has become the corner stone.
This is the work of the Lord,
  a marvel in our eyes.
The Lord has revealed himself, and given judgment. 9:17
The wicked are snared in the work of their own hands.
They dug a pit in my path   56:7
  but fell in it themselves.
The just will rejoice in the Lord   63:11
  and fly to him for refuge.
All the upright hearts will glory.
There are shouts of joy and victory   117:15
  in the tents of the just.

Alleluia!   110:1,2
I will thank the Lord with all my heart
  in the meeting of the just and their assembly.
Great are the works of the Lord;
  to be pondered by all who love them.

SILENT PRAYER

Lord, deepen my faith.
Though I see no wounds, I too can say, 'My Lord and
my God.'

MEDITATION

Risen Lord, you are the cornerstone, the key point of
reference, in our lives. You share your divinity with us
whom you made from clay; only with you and in you
are we truly alive to ourselves and to others. Grant us
the grace of fidelity as we build a spiritual house in our
souls. Let us lay a firm foundation with stones of faith
held fast by reverence and awe. When the floods of
faint-heartedness come and the gales of scepticism blow
and beat against the house, it will not fall. It is founded
on the rock of faith.

O Lord, we see your life on earth rooted in history
'under Pontius Pilate', but we perceive more: you are
God without beginning or end.

Deep in your wounds may we find shelter.

SILENT PRAYER

Jesus was crucified, died and was buried.
He descended to the dead.
On the third day he rose again.

THE WORD OF LOVE   Rom 6:8-11

If we have died with Christ, we believe that we shall
also live with him. For we know that Christ being
raised from the dead will never die again; death, no
longer has dominion over him. The death he died he
died to sin, once for all, but the life he lives he lives to
God. So you also must consider yourselves dead to sin
and alive to God in Christ Jesus.

All authority
has been given to me

THE WORD IN THE GOSPEL   Matt 28:18

Jesus came and said to the disciples, 'All authority in heaven and on earth has been given to me.'

THE WORD IN THE PSALMS

High above the nations is the Lord,   112:4
     above the heavens his glory.
The Lord's revelation to my Master: 109:1,2
     'Sit on my right:
     I will put your foes beneath your feet.'
The Lord will wield from Zion your scepter of power;
     rule in the midst of all your foes.
The Lord has set his sway in heaven   102:19
     and his kingdom is ruling over all.

My God, awake! You will give judgment.   7:7
You girded me with strength for battle;   17:40,41,44-46
     you made my enemies fall beneath me,
     you made my foes take flight;
     those who hated me I destroyed.
You saved me from the feuds of the people
     and put me at the head of the nations.
Foreign nations came to me cringing:
     foreign nations faded away.
     They came trembling out of their strongholds.
     People unknown to me served me:
     when they heard of me they obeyed me.
Arise, O God, judge the earth.   81:8

'Be still and know that I am God,   45:11
     supreme among the nations, supreme on the earth!'

SILENT PRAYER

     O key of David, what you close no one can open;
     what you open no one can close.

MEDITATION

King and law-giver, we acknowledge your authority over our world, one which is relentlessly questioning all authority. We know that you are saying: 'Come. Follow me.' If left alone, our response can only be at best hesitant and bungling; if animated by your strength, you alone can give expression to our potential as free, responsible persons. To obey your command gives each a unique vocation. It is the martyrs following in your footsteps who are special witnesses to the holiness of your truth-filled decrees.

Lord Jesus, we recognise that your authority safeguards the integrity of the human person and condemns homicide, genocide, abortion and euthanasia. May we always stand firm against attempts to coerce the human spirit; may we never fail to respect the personal dignity of others and rejoice in your truth and love.

SILENT PRAYER

May we respond to your authority which is truth.
Our response will carry us along the path of true freedom.

THE WORD OF LOVE   Dan 7:13,14

I saw in the night visions,
    and behold, with the clouds of heaven
    there came one like a son of man,
    and he came to the Ancient of Days
    and was presented before him.
And to him was given dominion
    and glory and kingdom,
    that all peoples, nations and languages
    should serve him;
    his dominion is an everlasting dominion.

'Make disciples of all nations'

THE WORD IN THE GOSPEL   Matt 28:18,19

Jesus came and said to his disciples, . . . 'Go therefore
and make disciples of all nations.'

THE WORD IN THE PSALMS

The Lord said to me . . .   2:7,8
'Ask and I shall bequeath you the nations,
    put the end of the earth in your possession.'
I will thank you, Lord, among the peoples,   107:4,5
    among the nations I will praise you,
    for your love reaches to the heavens
    and your truth to the skies.

Let the sea and all within it, thunder;   97:7-9
    the world and all its peoples.
Let the rivers clap their hands
    and the hills ring out their joy
    at the presence of the Lord; for he comes,
    he comes to rule the earth.
They shall worship him, all the mighty   21:30,28,29
    of the earth;
    before him shall bow down all who go down
    to the dust.
All the earth shall remember and return to the Lord,
    all families of the nations worship before him
    for the kingdom is the Lord's;
    he is ruler of the nations.

'O give thanks to the Lord for he is good;   106:1-3
    for his love is without end.'
Let them say this, the Lord's redeemed,
    whom he redeemed from the hand of the foe
    and gathered from far-off lands,
    from the east and west, north and south.
O praise the Lord, all you nations,   116:1
acclaim him all you peoples!

SILENT PRAYER

The word of the Lord is alive and active.
Is it so in me?

MEDITATION

One dark night as St Benedict prayed the whole world
appeared to be gathered up before his eyes in what
seemed like a single brilliant ray of light. Contemplating
God, his soul was so enlarged that the whole world
could be perceived at a glance. Our own familiarity with
pictures of our planet taken in outer space makes this
vision one to which we can easily relate.

Lord Jesus, we pray that the technological tools
which may evangelise all nations may be used as you
would wish. May satellite radio stations beam the Good
News of Love to every part of the globe. Let us always
remember that the missionary experience of two
millennia confirms that love is patient and kind.

O risen Christ, you are the fruitful vine and we are
your branches.

SILENT PRAYER

May each nation become one with Christ and so
yield its fruit.

THE WORD OF LOVE   Rev 5:9,10

You are worthy to take the scroll and to open its seals,
for you were slaughtered and by your blood you
ransomed for God saints from every tribe and language
and people and nation; you have made them to be a
kingdom and priests serving our God, and they will
reign on earth.

111

'I am with you always'

THE WORD IN THE GOSPEL Matt 28:18,20

And Jesus came and said to them, . . . 'Lo, I am with you always, to the close of the age.'

THE WORD IN THE PSALMS

Let this be written for ages to come 101:19
 that a people yet unborn may praise the Lord.
He shall endure like the sun and the moon 71:5
 from age to age.
His works are justice and truth: 110:7,8
 his precepts are all of them sure,
 standing firm for ever and ever:
 they are made in uprightness and truth.

Walk through Zion, walk all round it; 47:13-15
 count the number of its towers
 that you may tell the next generation
 that such is our God,
 our God for ever and always.
 It is he who leads us.

I will bless you day after day 144:2,4,5,7
 and praise your name for ever.
Age to age shall proclaim your works,
 shall declare your mighty deeds,
 shall speak of your splendour and glory,
 tell the tale of your wonderful works.
Age to age shall ring out your justice.
Let me tell of your power to all ages, 70:18,19
 praise your strength and justice to the skies,
 tell of you who have worked such wonders.
O God, who is like you?

Blessed be the Lord, the God of Israel 40:14
from age to age. Amen. Amen.

SILENT PRAYER

Christ today and tomorrow, the beginning and the end.
Loving Redeemer we are utterly dependent on you.

MEDITATION

The Paschal candle burns brightly during the Easter
Vigil service; the date of the year and the Greek letters,
'Alpha' and 'Omega' inscribed on it tell us that to Christ
belongs all time and all the ages. O happy fault (O felix
culpa), O necessary sin of Adam which gained for us the
abiding presence of our Emmanuel. May our gratitude
assume the eminently practical form of unceasing trust
in the Word and of joyful cultivation of the eternal
values.

Grant us, Lord, the grace of daily discernment as we
are bombarded by the secular voices of the mass media.
News – what constitutes it and the 'how' of its coverage
– is a rapidly changing kaleidoscope, but the good news
of Christ is alive for ever.

SILENT PRAYER

O Risen Christ, you are our stability.
Glory and power to you, now and through every
century for ever. Amen.

THE WORD OF LOVE   Rev 1:17c-18

'I am the first and the last, and the living one; I died,
and behold I am alive for evermore, and I have the keys
of Death and Hades.

Jesus ascended into heaven

THE WORD IN THE GOSPEL   Luke 24:50,51

Then Jesus led them out as far as Bethany, and lifting
up his hands he blessed them. While he blessed them,
he parted from them, and was carried up into heaven.

THE WORD IN THE PSALMS

O God, arise above the heavens;   56:6
    may your glory shine on earth!

Kingdoms of the earth, sing to God, praise the Lord 67:33,34
    who rides on the heavens, the ancient heavens.
All peoples, clap your hands,   46:2
    cry to God with shouts of joy!
It was the Lord who made the heavens,   95:5,6
    his are majesty and state and power
    and splendour in his holy place.
Come, acknowledge the power of God.   67:35
    His glory is on Israel; his might is in the skies.

God goes up with shouts of joy,   46:6,7
    the Lord goes up with trumpet blast.
Sing praise for God, sing praise,
    sing praise to our king, sing praise.
O sing to the Lord, make music to his name;   67:5
    make a highway for him who rides on the clouds.
Rejoice in the Lord, exult at his presence.
O gates, lift high your heads;   23:7
    grow higher ancient doors.
Let him enter the king of glory.

You have gone up on high; you have taken captives, 67:19
    receiving men and women in tribute, O God,
    even those who rebel, into your dwelling, O Lord.
You, Lord are eternally on high.   91:9

SILENT PRAYER

Lord God, Lamb of God, you are seated at the right hand of the Father: receive our prayer.

MEDITATION

Heaven is an acquired taste. May we acquire it! Christ has ascended, taking captives, even sinners like ourselves, into his dwelling. 'The chariots of God', 'thousands upon thousands', are filled with families of saints. The celestial highway is to be taken by those who are free. Let us exert ourselves to become less unworthy. Since Christ is our head and we are his body, he is with us and even now we can be with him.

At your Ascension, Lord, you promised us the Holy Spirit, the comforter. Grant that the same Spirit may so permeate our lives that our witness to your risen glory may be strengthened.

We believe that you are drawing us all to yourself, and the nearer we come to you the less we shall be separated from one another.

SILENT PRAYER

His kingdom of glory will have no end.
Am I ready to greet him when he comes again?

THE WORD OF LOVE   Heb 8:1b,2

We have such a high priest, one who is seated at the right hand of the throne of the majesty in the heavens, a minister in the sanctuary and the true tent that the Lord, and not any mortal, has set up.

The disciples worshipped him

THE WORD IN THE GOSPEL   Luke 24:52,53

The disciples worshipped him, and returned to
Jerusalem with great joy, and were continually in the
temple blessing God.

THE WORD IN THE PSALMS

Bring an offering and enter his courts,   95:8,9
   worship the Lord in his temple.
The Lord is great and worthy to be praised   47:1,2
   in the city of our God,
Mount Zion, true pole of the earth,
   the great King's city!
The Lord is great in Zion.   98:2,3
He is supreme over all the peoples.
Let them praise his name, so terrible and great.
He is holy, full of power.

O God, we ponder your love   47:10,11
   within your temple.
Your praise, O God, like your name
   reaches to the ends of the earth.
We give thanks to you, O God,   74:2
   we give thanks and call upon your name.
We recount your wonderful deeds.
The foe is destroyed, eternally ruined.   9:7
   You uprooted their cities; their memory has perished.
For the sake of your temple high in Jerusalem 67:30
   may kings come to you bringing their tribute.

Blessed be the Lord, God of Israel,   71:18,19
   who alone works wonders,
   ever blessed his glorious name.
   Let his glory fill the earth.
   Amen! Amen!

SILENT PRAYER

May our lives today be honest and holy as we await
the happiness to come.

MEDITATION

With hearts bubbling over with the glorious experience of
what they had heard and seen of Christ, the disciples
worshipped God. May we too experience something of
their fervour and share it with others through a sincerity
of heart which is infectious.

In our worship let us savour words of quality which
highlight the holiness of God who transcends all creation
by the sublime nature of his unparalleled power.
Similarly let us enjoy music which uplifts the soul – either
the timelessness of Gregorian plainchant or the excellence
of later compositions.

Despite the noise of our world, let us not be afraid to
utilise silence, a silence in which the soul may expand.
Lord, grant that we may worship you in spirit and in
truth through the integrity of our lives.

SILENT PRAYER

Let us join in continuous prayer with Mary, the mother
of Jesus.
May we sanctify each hour.

THE WORD OF LOVE   Tobit 13:15-18

Let my soul praise God the great King . . .
for Jerusalem will be built with sapphires and emeralds,
    her walls with precious stones,
    and her towers and battlements with pure gold.
The streets of Jerusalem will be paved with beryl and
ruby and stones of Ophir:
    all her lanes will cry 'Hallelujah!' and will give praise,
    saying, 'Blessed is God, who has exalted you for ever.'

117

ACKNOWLEDGEMENTS

Gospel Texts
From the New Revised Standard Version Bible,
copyright 1946, 1952 and 1971 by the Division of
Christian Education of the National Council of the
Churches of Christ in the USA.
Used by permission.

Psalms
Taken from *The Grail Psalms*,
published by HarperCollins Publishers,
and used by permission of A.P. Watt Ltd
on behalf of The Grail, England.